World War I Battlefields

A Travel Guide to the Western Front

Sites • Museums • Memorials

the Bradt Travel Guide

John Ruler & Emma Thomson

edition

1

www.bradtguide

Bradt Travel Guides Ltd, UK

AUTHORS

John Ruler is a member of the British Guild of Travel Writers and the Outdoor Writers Guild. He is a Nord-Pas de Calais specialist and writes about the area frequently for monthly magazines.

Emma Thomson is an award-winning travel writer and a member of the British Guild of Travel Writers. She writes for international magazines, newspapers and guidebook publishers (online and print) and was shortlisted for Young Travel Writer of the Year at the British Travel Press Awards. She lives in Aalst, Belgium.

First edition published March 2014

Bradt Travel Guides Ltd
IDC House, The Vale, Chalfont St Peter, Bucks SL9 9RZ, England
www.bradtguides.com

ISBN: 978 1 84162 484 6 (print)

British Library Cataloguing in Publication Data
A catalogue record for this book is available from the British Library

Photographs Aisne Tourisme (AT): Franck Viltart (FV/AT), FX Dessirier (FXD/AT), Jan D'Hondt-BAD (JD-BAD/AT), OT Fère-en-Tardenois (OTFT/AT), S Lefebvre (SL/AT); Alamy: Peter Chadwick (PC/A); Collections of Ville de Mons (CVM); Doug Goodman (DG); Emma Thomson (ET); Historial de la Grande Guerre-Péronne (Somme): Paul Hoffmann (PH/HGGP); (MPP); Lawrence Bitterly (LB); Le Nord Tourisme (LNT); Pas-de-Calais Tourisme (PCT); Somme Tourisme (ADRT80): AB (AB/ST), AD (AD/ST), CP (CP/ST), PC (PC/ST); Visit Flanders (VF): Hans Kerrinckx (HK/VF), Memorial Museum Passchendaele 1917 (MMP/VF), Milo-Profi Photography (MPP/VF), Toerisme Ieper (TI/VF), Westtoer (W/VF); Velvet (V); Verdun Tourisme: JM Perraux/Ville de Verdun (JMP/VV/VT); Volksbunde Deutsche Kriegsgräberfürsorge (VDK); WBT-JP Remy (WBT-JPR); Wikipedia (W)

Front cover Corn poppy fields, Flanders (PC/A)
Flanders version front cover Military cemetery, Flanders (VF)
Back cover Gravestones in Tyne Cot Cemetery (MPP/VF); Soldiers in front of a ruined church (MMP/VF)
Title page Ypres (TI/VF); Étaples Military Cemetery (PCT); Memorial to the American 42nd Division, Aisne (OTFT/AT)
Part openers Page 1: Horse and cart outside Ypres (MMP/VF); Page 11: German zeppelin (MMP/VF); Page 39: Nurses aiding soldiers after a gas attack, The Somme (PH/HGGP)
Maps David McCutcheon FBCart.S

Layout from the authors' disc by Ian Spick, Bradt Travel Guides Ltd
Production managed by Jellyfish Print Solutions; printed in the UK
Digital conversion by the Firsty Group

Contents

LIST OF MAPS

KEY TO MAP SYMBOLS

——	The Western Front	✝	Church/chapel
∙∙∙∙ ∙∙ ∙∙	International border	⬚	Cemetery
▓▓▓	Motorway	🗼	Memorial/statue
═══	Main road	❄	Viewpoint
═══	Secondary road	🚂	Historic railway
——	Other road	○	Crater
▫▫▫▫	Railway	⬛	Bunker
✈	Airport	▬	Minefields
P	Parking	✕	Battlefield
ⓘ	Tourist information	♧	Notable tree/woodland feature
⊞	Historic/important building	•	Other point of interest
🏰	Tower/fortress	∿∿∿	Trenches
🏛	Memorial archway	▓▓	Urban area
🏺	Museum		

Introduction

When Germany declared war on France on 3 August 1914, what was meant to be a quick war 'over by Christmas' turned into four years of attrition. Both sides dug in and a line of trenches stretching from the North Sea to the Swiss border created a line known as the Western Front. From 1914 to 1918 this line only fluctuated by a few miles in either direction as the Germans fought to reach the North Sea (to cut off Allied supply routes) and the Allies (the British, French, Australians, Canadians and Americans) attempted to push them back. By the end of World War I, total human casualties numbered over 37 million – of which over 16 million died and 20 million were wounded. It ranks as the sixth-deadliest conflict in human history.

From 2014 to 2018, Great War centenary celebrations and remembrances will be taking place across the world, but nowhere with more verve than France and Belgium where the battles were played out. This practical guide covers all the main cemeteries, memorials and museums in these countries, as well as practical information on how to reach them, how to research a lost family member and the best guided tours. It is tailored specifically for visitors, both young and old, planning pilgrimages to visit relatives that fought in the war or for those just wanting to learn more about this dark period of history – 'Lest we forget'.

Acknowledgements

Thanks and gratitude to our Bradt project editor Kelly Randell, cartographer David McCutcheon, contributor Doug Goodman, and the following regional experts who checked the text for us: Benoît Diéval, Delphine Bartier, Florence Tabart, Aude Carrier and Veerle Viane. Also many thanks to contributing editor Philippe Barbour for editing the French section of the text and James B Randell for checking historical information.

DEDICATION

Dedicated to Herbert John Ruler, who died in France aged 18, and to all who perished in the Great War

Part One

GENERAL INFORMATION

WORLD WAR I TIMELINE

1914

28 June–27 July The assassination of Archduke Franz Ferdinand by a Bosnian Serb assassin, Gazrilo Princip, in Sarajevo leads to Kaiser Wilhelm II promising Germany's support in the event of retaliation against Serbia.

28 July Austria–Hungary declares war on Serbia and British fleets are ordered to war bases.

3 August Germany declares war on France and invades Belgium.

4 August At 23.00 Britain declares war on Germany.

23 August The first major battle begins (and ends) at Mons in Belgium with the British forced to retreat in the face of greater German manpower and artillery (see box, page 35).

22 September–end of November The first battles of Picardy, Albert, Arras and Ypres take place.

26 & 29 October Nieuwpoort sluice gates are opened to flood the plain and halt the German advance (see box, page 34).

1915

25 September Start of the Battle of Loos (see box, page 58). British soldiers, forced to pull off inefficient masks, choke on their own gas as it blows back across the lines. Battle ends on 6 October.

German soldiers keep watch in a stone-walled trench, the Somme (PH/HGGP)

1916

21 February A huge loss by the French at the Battle of Verdun (see box, page 88), the longest of the war, leads the British to start the Battle of the Somme as a diversionary tactic.

1 July Battle of the Somme begins (see box, page 66). Over a period of 4½ months the British Army, despite capturing key positions, advances only a few miles before winter sets in and fighting ceases.

1917

7–14 June Battle of Messines – regarded as one of Britain's greatest war victories (see box, page 29).

31 July The final phase of the Third Battle of Ypres in Belgium grinds on into the autumn and winter (see box, page 22).

20 November Battle of Cambrai sees 450 tanks pitted against the German Front Line.

1918

15 July Second Battle of the Marne in Champagne shows signs of German collapse.

8 August Allies' advance is successful.

4 October Germany seeks an armistice.

9 November Kaiser abdicates.

11 November Armistice is signed in a railway carriage in the Oise region on the 11th hour of the 11th day of the 11th month. World War I ends.

2

Practical Information

GETTING THERE AND AWAY

BY FERRY The faster Eurostar and Eurotunnel services have heavily eclipsed travel by boat, but for families it remains the cheapest option. **P&O Ferries** (*0871 664 6464; www. poferries.com*) and **MyFerryLink** (*0844 248 2100; www.myferrylink. com*) both operate a Dover–Calais route and P&O also runs an overnight Hull–Zeebrugge route. **DFDS Seaways** (*0871 574 7235; www.dfdsseaways.co.uk*) operates a Dover–Dunkirk route.

EUROTUNNEL (LE SHUTTLE) (*0844 335 3535; www.eurotunnel.com*) is a high-speed car train that runs from Folkestone to Calais. Journeys take 35 minutes. Book early and travel outside peak times for the best rates.

BY TRAIN
From the UK
Eurostar (*0843 218 6186; www.eurostar.com*) runs up to nine services a day from London St Pancras to Lille, Paris or Brussels via the Channel Tunnel. Advance booking essential; the earlier you book the greater chance of a cheap fare. If you're travelling to Belgium be sure to select the 'Any Belgian Station' option from the 'Belgium' drop-down menu when booking online, as this allows you to travel on to Ypres or Poperinge, for example, for free.

From France, Germany, Luxembourg and the Netherlands
Thalys (*0032 (0)70 79 79 79; www.thalys.com*) provides an inter-Europe network with connections between all major western European cities. Be aware that booking over the phone incurs a €7 administration fee.

BY COACH
Eurolines (*0871 781 8178; www.eurolines.co.uk*) operate four daily departures from London Victoria coach station to Brussels, Bruges and Lille. The journey takes approximately nine hours and includes a Dover–Calais ferry crossing. **Megabus** (*0900 160 0900; uk.megabus.com*) now run twice-daily services from a host of UK cities to Brussels and Paris.

GETTING AROUND

BY CAR Many of the World War I battlefields, memorials and cemeteries are located in the countryside so it really helps to have your own car. Remember to drive on the right, take sufficient cash to pay at French motorway tollbooths (*péages*) and observe *priorité à droite* (give way to the right on secondary roads and roundabouts). In Belgium, it's illegal to drive without carrying headlamp adapters, a warning triangle, reflective vest, first-aid kit and fire extinguisher in your car, so be prepared.

BY TRAIN
In France *with thanks to French rail travel expert Peter Mills.*
There is an extensive network of local trains serving towns both large and small, and the French national rail network, **SNCF** (www.sncf.com/en), operates a number of different types of services. **TGV** (Train à Grande Vitesse; www.tgv.com/en) is a high-speed, long

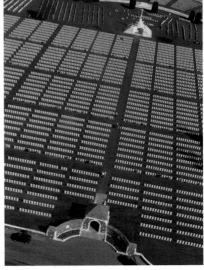
Tyne Cot Cemetery (W/VF)

distance service (booking prior to travel is essential), and **OUIGO** (http://ventes. ouigo.com) is SNCF's new high-speed, low-fare service. **TER** (Transport Express Régional; www.ter-sncf.com) is a network of regional trains – there's no need to book in advance; simply buy a ticket at the station. Timetable leaflets (fiches horaires) are available in all stations. Intercités (www.intercites.sncf.com) is a classic French rail service with medium- and long-distance services. Bikes are allowed on most trains, but check individual websites for details. For full information on all aspects of rail travel in France, visit http://uk.voyages-sncf.com/en or call ✆ 0844 848 5848.

In Belgium The national rail network is run by **SNCB-NMBS** (✆ *02 528 28 28; www.belgianrail.be*). Tickets can be bought online, at the station or on board as a last resort. Fares start at €7.50 for a second-class return ticket. Bicycles are now allowed on trains free of charge.

BY BIKE Numerous local tourist offices rent bikes and have specially tailored World War I bike trail maps for sale. These have been listed under individual towns.

TOURIST INFORMATION

There are no tourist offices for Flanders as yet in Australia, Canada, Ireland and New Zealand.

FRANCE

Australia French Tourist Bureau, 25 Bligh St – level 13, Sydney, NSW 2000 (this bureau also serves New Zealand)
Belgium 21 Ave de la Toison d'Or, 1050 Brussels
Canada 1800 Av McGill Collège, Bureau 1010, Montreal, Québec H3A 3J6
Germany Zeppelinallee 37, D-60325 Frankfurt
Ireland 30 Upper Merrion St, Dublin 2
The Netherlands Prinsengracht 670, 1017 KX, Amsterdam

UK (London office) Lincoln Hse, 300 High Holborn, London, WC1V 7JH; ✆ 090 68 244 123 (60p/min at all times); ℮ info.uk@franceguide. com; www.franceguide.com; ⏱ 10.00–16.00 Mon–Fri. Click on Nord-Pas de Calais; information includes last-minute accommodation availability from hotels & campsites, with links to regional & local websites.
USA 825 Third Av, New York, NY 10022 & 9454 Wilshire Bd – Suite 21, Beverley Hills, CA 90212

Belgium Visit Flanders: Rue du Marché aux Herbes 61, Brussels; +322 504 03 90; www.toerismevlaanderen.be; Visit Brussels: Rue Royale 2, Brussels; +322 513 89 70; www.visitbrussels.be

France 21 Bd des Capucines, Paris; +33 1 4742 41 18; www.belgique-tourisme.be

Germany 46 Cäcilienstrasse, 50667 Köln; +49 221 270 97 52; www.flandern.com

Netherlands 86 Koninginnegracht, 2514 AJ Den Haag; +31 70 416 81 10; www.toerisme-vlaanderen.nl

UK 1a Cavendish Sq, London W1G 0LD; +44 020 7307 7738; www.visitflanders.co.uk

USA 300 East 42nd St, 14th Flr, New York, NY 10017; +1 212 758 8130; www.visitbelgium.com

BATTLEFIELD TOURS

A huge range of battlefield tours is available. We've listed UK-based outfits below and France- or Belgium-specific companies in the relevant chapters. In all cases book early; tours are filling up fast ahead of the centenary.

Advance Battlefield Tours 01728 603 645; www.advancebattlefieldtours.co.uk. Small tailor-made tours taking in main tourist areas, with advice on tracing relatives.

Anglia Tours 01376 574 130; www.angliatours.co.uk. Coach tours for schools & special-interest groups from churches & sports clubs to parents' associations.

Back-Roads Touring Co. Battlefield Tours 020 898 7099; www.backroadstouring.co.uk. Include battlefield visits as part of a wider programme using 16-seater mini-coaches.

Bartletts Battlefield Journeys Ltd 01507 523 128; www.battlefields.co.uk. Tours in AC people carriers for groups of 7 or under, or medium-sized coach for groups of 10–15.

Battle Honours 01438 791 020; www.battle-honours.co.uk. Concentrate on off-the-beaten-track walking tours for groups up to 16. Director & joint owner Clive Harris served in the Royal Signals. Canadian office too.

Battlefields By Bike 01636 302 123; www.battlefieldsbybike.co.uk. Offers a whole host of cycling trips that last a day, w/end or longer.

Bike & Culture Flanders www.bikeandcultureflanders.com. Family-run business offers a 4-day World War I bike tour, inc visits to Ghent & Bruges. You stay in 4-star hotels & all transfers, equipment & entrance fees are included in the price.

Bird Battlefield Tours 020 8752 0956/01243 789077; www.birdbattlefieldtours.com. Tours encourage dinner-table discussions for groups of 4–16, inclusive of ferry or flights.

Clevelode Battlefield Tours 01684 311 257; www.clevelode-battletours.com. Run by David Craig, a retired British Army officer with an MA in World War I studies. Bespoke small group/family tours a speciality, as well as school travel.

The Cultural Experience 0845 475 1815; www.theculturalexperience.com. Offers coach & other bespoke tours for 6–20 people on a variety of topics.

Dr Thomson's Tours 01227 455 922; www.drttours.co.uk. Tours, led by Dr Andrew Thomson, who has a PhD in history, take up to 5 people in air-conditioned Citroën C8 minivan or rental vehicles.

The Last Post, Menin Gate, Ypres (MPP/VF)

First port of call is the **Commonwealth War Graves Commission** (*2 Marlow Rd, Maidenhead, Berks SL6 7DX; ☎ 01628 634221; www.cwgc.org*). They can now locate online an actual grave within a specific cemetery, or the name commemorated on a World War I memorial.

If you have only a surname to go on, especially a common one, use the Advance Search option on the website listed above to avoid looking through a long list. This narrows the choice, provided you know in which armed service your relative served along with perhaps rank, regiment or service number.

Initial homework helps too: photographs, medals, diaries and letters, even stories passed down in the family, are all pieces in a puzzle which help pinpoint a particular grave or memorial site.

National archive collections, military museums and libraries, newspapers and photo libraries likewise help plug gaps, as do local archives, village memorials and church records. Relatives looking for German soldiers should visit www.volksbund.be and you can search for Belgian casualties at www.inflandersfields.be.

Ecosse Tours Ltd ☎ 0141 416 1915; www.ecossetours.co.uk. Scottish company (tours start there) with an eclectic selection of expert guides, from a Glasgow-born writer to an archaeologist, who lead bespoke coach tours, including those for schools.

Eyewitness Tours ☎ 01306 880 960; www.eyewitnesstours.com. Led by former history teacher Andy Thompson who has been studying war & conflict for 40 years. Tours hone in on the lives of individual soldiers.

Holts Tours Battlefields and History ☎ 01293 865 000; www.holts.co.uk. Founded by Tonie & Valmai Holt back in 1975, the company is now part of Titan Travel with departures from London Victoria coach station.

In the Footsteps ☎ 01989 565 599; www.inthefootsteps.com. Tailor-made tours by experts in a variety of topics.

Kimber Battlefield Tours ☎ 07710 415458; www.kimberbattlefieldtours.co.uk. Launched by Paul Trickett, a former Royal Marine musician

with BA & MA degrees in history, & assisted by a former army colleague, the company offers 4- or 5-day Ypres tours, 4- or 6-day Somme tours as well as 4- or 6-day Normandy tours.

Leger Holidays Guided Battlefield Coach Tours ☎ 0844 504 6306; www.visitbattlefield.co.uk. 3–4 - night tours for those familiar with Leger's European programme with feeder pick-up points.

On The Go Tours ☎ 0207 371 1117; www.onthegotours.com. Offer 2 4-day tours, focusing on ANZAC sites, travelling via coach or Eurostar.

Remembrance Travel (formerly Poppy Travel) ☎ 020 3207 2321; www.remembrancetravel.org.uk. This specialist travel division of the Royal British Legion provides a unique insight into major military sites. In 2013 they partnered with Newmarket Travel to deliver their Journey of Remembrance programme.

Rifleman Tours ☎ 01908 617264; www.riflemantours.co.uk. Run by husband-&-wife team Tony & Allison Eden, who offer tours for

There are dozens of Great War anniversary events taking place in 2014, but we don't have room to include them all here. For an up-to-date list, please visit Bradt's *World War I Battlefield's* updates website: www.bradtupdates.com/WWI.

12–18 people, from the first-time battlefield visitor to the serious researcher.

Skylark Battlefield Tours 01354 696 779; www.skylarkbattlefieldtours.co.uk. Concentrate on bespoke tours for schools, colleges, special-interest groups, military personnel & Combined Cadet Forces.

Spirit of History 01883 744 342; www.spiritofhistory.co.uk. Run by former history teachers with over 23 years' experience of organising school & adult trips. They also offer help researching family graves.

Spirit of Remembrance 01634 233785/01420 475567; www.spiritofremembrance.com. Bespoke tours backed by Paul Julius, founder of Medway Travel. Group tours manager & chief guide is Colonel Christopher Newbould CBE.

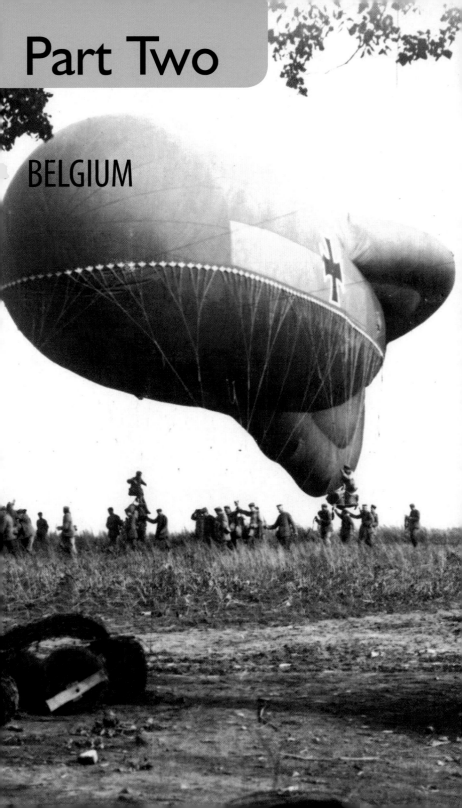

Part Two

BELGIUM

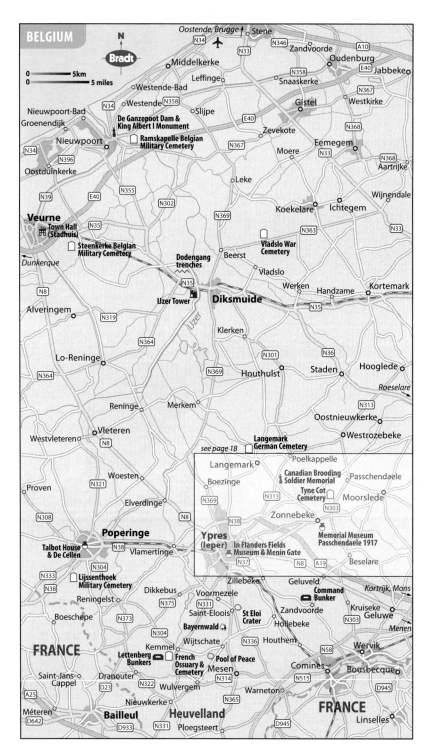

3

Ypres and the Ypres Salient

YPRES (IEPER)

Ypres – or 'Wipers' as it was nicknamed by British soldiers – is a relatively small town with a very famous history. War arrived here on 7 October 1914 when 10,000 German troops entered the town, kidnapped the burgomaster, stole 62,000 francs from the city coffers and demanded the local bakers prepare 8,000 loaves of bread to feed the soldiers. The next morning they released the burgomaster and marched west towards Vlamertinghe. The Germans never entered the city again and residents felt safe enough to stay put until May 1915 when chlorine gas was deployed on the battlefields. As the war progressed, Ypres became a strategic defence point of the Ypres Salient (see page 17) and was battered by artillery fire. When locals returned at the end of the war, it was barely recognisable. It's said you could sit on horseback and look over the town without a single building interrupting your view.

GETTING THERE AND AWAY

By car If travelling from Calais or Dunkerque, leave the E40 at exit 14 and follow N8 south to Ypres (*53km; approx 50mins*). Remember, Ypres is known as 'Ieper' in Flanders and can change on road signs. From Lille, follow the A25/E42 west and then join the N58 leading north past Armentieres; after a few miles turn left onto N336 towards Ypres (*40km; approx 40mins*).

By train Brussels-Zuid/Bruxelles-Midi (*41mins past the hour Mon–Fri, 36mins past the hour Sat–Sun; 1hr 45mins*); Brugge via Kortrijk (*32mins past the hour daily; 1hr49mins*); Gent via Kortrijk (*9mins past the hour daily; 1hr12mins*). Trains from Lille to Ypres require about four changes; consult www.b-europe.co.uk for times.

TOURIST INFORMATION

Ypres Tourist Office Lakenhalle, 34 Grote Markt; ☏ 057 23 92 20; www.toerismeieper.be; ⏱ 09.00–17.00 Mon–Fri, 10.00–17.00 Sat–Sun. A large well-equipped office that can organise hotel bookings & battlefield tours, & sells self-guided tour maps for bikes & cars (see box, page 16).

GUIDED TOURS

Battlefield Exploration 21 Remi Ghesquièrestraat, 8940 Geluwe; ☏ 0486 968 307; e info@battlefieldexploration.com; www. battlefieldexploration.com. Offers a clutch of small-group 3hr tours (€30pp) of Ypres Salient,

Messines Ridge & Menin Road, plus detailed on-site battlefield accounts. Trips further afield & pick-ups from your hotel possible.
Camalou Guided Battlefield Tours ☏ 057 20 43 42; e info@visit-ypres.be; www.visit-ypres.be.

In Flanders Fields Museum, Ypres (MPP/VF)

2-man team who offer a very thorough British-tailored full-day tour taking in all the sights; €105pp, inc lunch & all entrance fees.

Cavells Guided Battlefield Tours 0479 80 64 26; info@cavells.be; www.cavells.be. Local B&B that runs a 2hr walking tour of Ypres centre (€20pp), as well as North & South Salient tours (€40pp each).

Flanders Battlefield Tours 057 36 04 60; info@ypres-fbt.com; www.ypres-fbt.com. Englishwoman Genevra Charsley & her Flemish husband study & conduct research all winter, so come summertime their tours are the city's best. Very knowledgeable, friendly & accommodating. Their standard tour includes Essex Farm, Tyne Cot, Hill 62, Vancouver Corner & the New Zealand Memorial (1 Apr–31 Oct 10.00–12.30 daily; 1 Nov–31 Mar on request; €30pp). The larger North & South Salient tours cost €35pp. Their silver minibuses depart from the public bus stop on Grote Markt.

Frontline Tours 057 85 99 35; info@ frontline-tours.com; www.frontline-tours.com. Has a selection of 2hr tours explaining the battles of Messines & Passchendaele, €25pp.

Lest We Forget Battlefield Tours 32/2 Surmont de Volsberghestraat; 057 36 01 34; info@lestweforgettours.com; www. lestweforgettours.com. Small outfit offering a variety of half-day Ypres Salient tours & Ypres city centre tours from €45pp. Max group size of 4, so very intimate.

Over the Top Tours 41 Meensestraat; 057 42 43 20; tours@overthetoptours.be; www. overthetoptours.be. Run daily morning & afternoon tours of the Ypres Salient, which depart at 09.30 & return at 13.30 & cost €40pp, & a full-day tour of the Somme, which departs

WIPERS TIMES

In 1916, the 12th Battalion Sherwood Foresters from Nottingham and Derbyshire Regiment stumbled across an abandoned printing press while stationed in Ypres. One of their men was able to salvage it and they printed off a trial paper, calling it *Wipers Times* after the British nickname for Ypres. Filled with poems and hugely satirical, it included entries such as:

WEATHER FORECAST:

5 to 1	Mist
11 to 2	East Wind or Frost
8 to 1	Chlorine

The trench magazine became hugely popular and, in 2013, the BBC broadcast a dramatisation about its creation.

at 08.00 & returns at 17.45 & costs €90pp (min 4 people). Meet at the OTT bookshop beside the Menin Gate.

Protea Guide Battlefields Tours ✆ 057 46 63 39; ✉ info@theprotea.be; www.theprotea-ypres. be. Local B&B that runs tours & will do grave research for you prior to arrival.

Salient Tours British Grenadier Bookshop, 5 Meensestraat; ✆ 057 21 46 57; ✉ tours@ salienttours.be; www.salienttours.be. Their standard tour covers the whole Salient departs at daily 10.00 returns at 14.00 & costs €38pp. The Short Tour departs at 14.30 returns at 17.00 & costs €30pp & visits Hill 60, Bayernwald trenches & Bedford House cemetery. Longer Somme, Vimy Ridge & Arras tours available too.

WWI Battlefields Alive ✆ 0478 06 63 79; ✉ battlefields.alive@gmail.com; www.

ww1battlefieldsalive.com. Historian with 31-years of experience offers a selection of 4hr tours & will tailor tours as well. (€40pp).

Specialist tours

Alfa Flight www.alfaflight.be. See all the famous World War I sites from the air on this 60min flight; €345 price includes transfers to Kortrijk-Wevelgem International Airport & a max of 3 passengers.

Cycling the Western Front ✆ 0475 81 06 08; ✉ carl-ooghe@gmail.com; www. cyclingthewesternfront.co.uk. Rents out GPS systems that'll lead visitors around World War I sites (€10/day) & can arrange bike hire too, or offers guided bike tours lasting a day or week, taking in sites you request (€70pp/day).

WHAT TO SEE AND DO

In Flanders Fields Museum (*Grote Markt 34;* ✆ *057 23 92 20; www.inflandersfields. be;* ⏰ *1 Apr–15 Nov 10.00–18.00 daily; 16 Nov–31 Mar 10.00–17.00 Tue–Sun; adult/18–25/7–18 €9/5/4; W/A with help*) Located on the second floor of the Lakenhalle, this new high-tech museum centres around the 'poppy bracelet'. It's issued to you on arrival and then you input your name and place of birth and the computer selects personal stories of people from your town or county who participated in the war. You'll then be able to print or email the stories to your smartphone and create an itinerary to visit the areas where they fought. You can keep the bracelet as a souvenir and forgo the €1 deposit. Entry to the bell tower costs an extra €2, but is well worth it for the views overlooking famous battlegrounds. Be aware that it's a steep climb and not accessible to wheelchair users. It also has a **knowledge centre** (✆ *057 23 94 50;* ⏰ *10.00–12.30 &13.30–17.00 Mon–Fri*), which individuals can use to trace relatives.

Saint-George's Memorial Church (*Elverdingsestraat 1;* ✆ *057 21 56 86;* ⏰ *1 Apr–30 Sep 09.30–20.00 daily; 1 Oct–31 Mar 09.30–16.00 daily; free entry*) This unassuming church was designed by Sir Reginald Bloomfield – the architect responsible for the Menin Gate – in 1929. It's filled with brass plaques honouring fallen soldiers and furniture donated by the victims' families. The stained-glass windows dedicated to various individuals and regiments are moving too, especially the window on the right above the baptistry which remembers Captain Boyce Combe. He was killed on 11 November 1912 at the tender age of 26 and his name appears on the Menin Gate.

Visitors enjoy an exhibit at the In Flanders Fields Museum (MPP/VF)

Visiting sites where family members may have died in battle is emotional and for many a pilgrimage of sorts. If you'd prefer privacy, why not rent a bike and take off on your own? The tourist board sells two maps. The 28.5km *Mine Warfare: Messines Ridge 1917* and 35km *Ypres Salient* route (€3) uses Flanders's regional numbered cycling network. The accompanying booklet comes in English and has useful aerial photographs, diagrams and explanations of the various sites. Or, if you're feeling a bit more confident, the un-signposted circular 45km *Vredes* route (€2) departs from the Grote Markt and, among others, takes in Essex Farm Cemetery, Langemark, the Vancouver Corner, Tyne Cot and Hill 62. Explanations are in Dutch only.

If you don't fancy all that pedaling, take the car and follow the 82km *In Flanders Fields* route (€3), which takes in Poperinge, Messines and Zonnebeke, or the 70km *Ypres Salient* route.

Ramparts War Museum (*Rijselsestraat 208;* ✆ *057 20 02 36;* ☉ *10.30–20.00 Mon, Tue, Fri–Sun; €3*) Owned by the old-fashioned 't Klein Rijsel pub located next door, this small museum has a lovely private collection of war artefacts displayed in patiently recreated scenes of the trenches and bunkers. A short walk west will bring you to the Ramparts Commonwealth Cemetery.

Menin Gate (Meninpoort) (*Meensestraat; www.lastpost.be*) Erected in July 1927, the Menin Gate marks the spot where soldiers would leave town on their way to the Front Line. Carved into the interior walls are the names of 54,896 British and Commonwealth soldiers killed in World War I and whose graves are unknown.

Menin Gate, Ypres (W/VF)

Soldiers who went missing after 16 August 1917 have their names inscribed on the arches at Tyne Cot Cemetery (see page 23). As a mark of respect, the road is closed every evening at 20.00 and members of the local fire brigade sound their bugles. One member, Anton Deon, has been sounding his horn for over 57 years. Known as the 'Last Post', this tribute to the fallen has continued uninterrupted since 2 July 1928, except under German occupation during World War II when the ceremony was conducted in Brookwood Military Cemetery in Surrey. A verse from Laurence Binyon's poem 'For the Fallen' is usually read aloud too. On the 9 July 2015, the 30,000th 'Last Post' will be played.

THE YPRES SALIENT

A salient is a military defence line that bulges into enemy territory and is surrounded on three sides. The one which developed around the town of Ypres (Ieper) during World War I was a result of the failure of the German Schlieffen Plan. Their aim was to avoid fighting a war on two fronts by invading France, then capturing its sea ports and Paris, via Belgium, before Russian troops could mobilise on the East German border. The attack relied on speed and the element of surprise. The Germans lost both when they were caught unawares by the Belgian resistance who delayed German troops for over a month until French and British soldiers arrived. Both sides dug in: the Allies (British, French, Canadian and Belgians) defending the coastline and the Germans pushing towards it. Both sides built trenches in the soil that stretched for 400 miles from Nieuwpoort to the French/Swiss border, a line known as the Western Front. The contours of this line were established during the First Battle of Ypres when Allied forces fought the Germans for control of Ypres and won, securing the last major town that stood between the Germans and the coast.

Over the next four years, this line would barely move. Vicious trench warfare ensued with increasingly bloody (and muddy) battles being fought in a bid to reach ridges, like Tyne Cot and Hill 60, that would provide elevated views of the battlefield and enemy lines. Ever more ruthless tactics were employed to weaken the enemy, including the use of chlorine and mustard gases, and casualties soared, culminating in the Third Battle of Ypres (see box, page 22), which claimed the lives of over half a million soldiers. By the time the Armistice was signed on 11 November 1918, 1.5 billion shells had been fired on the Western Front and an estimated 750,000 soldiers had lost their lives in the Salient. The entire area was a wasteland of death, decay and liquid mud – the only sign of life was the flash of red poppies, whose long-dormant seeds had been brought to the surface. Today, the area is green once more and dotted with cemeteries honouring the fallen soldiers.

ESSEX FARM CEMETERY (*N38 & N369 crossroads; ⊕ daily; free entry; W/A with help*) Two kilometres north of Ypres city centre, the Essex Farm bunker sat 1,800m from the Front Line and was used as an Advance Dressing Station (ADS). It was here on 3 May 1915 that Canadian surgeon Lieutenant Colonel John McCrae penned one of the most notable poems of World War I, 'In Flanders Fields' (see box, page 19) after witnessing the death of his friend Alexis Helmer the day before. Helmer's name appears on panel ten of the Menin Gate. The poem was sent to *The Spectator* magazine in London, but rejected and eventually published by *Punch* on 8 December 1915. You can visit the bunkers where McCrae tended the wounded, and the adjacent cemetery, where you should look for the grave of rifleman Valentine Joseph Strudwick – he was killed by a shell two months before his 16th birthday.

THE YPRES SALIENT

0 ___ 1km
0 ___ 1 mile

Ypres city centre

Saint George's Memorial Church
Sint Maartenskathedraal
Over the Top Tours
Menin Gate (Meninpoort)
BOLLINGSTRAAT
British Grenadier Bookshop & Salient Tours
MENENSTRAAT
KORTE TORHOUTSTRAAT
OUDE HOUTMARKTSTRAAT
JANSENIUS STRAAT
Grote Markt
Flanders Battlefield Tour pick-up point
Lakenhalle
In Flanders Fields
Neermarkt
LANGE MEERSSTRAAT
Station

Moorslede
Waterdam
Slypskapelle
Strooiboom
Kelberg
Molenaarelst
N303
N303
Passchendaele
Tyne-Cot
Geluveld
Kortrijk
N8
Front Line November 1917
Tyne Cot Cemetery
Broodseinde
Memorial Museum Passchendaele 1917
Polygon Wood Cemetery
Buttes New British Cemetery
Zonnebeke
Front Line November 1917
Front Line November 1914
Front Line November 1914
Front Line November 1917
Westhoek
Poelkapelle, Guynemer Monument
ZONNEBEKESTRAAT
N332
Frenzenberg
A19
Fortuinhoek
N37
Sanctuary Wood Cemetery
Canadian Brooding Soldier Memorial
Langemark German Cemetery (800m)
Langemark
Hooge Crater
Hooge Crater Cemetery
N8
Hill 60 Memorial (100m)
Sint-Juliaan
N313
Front Line May 1915
ZONNEBEKESEWEG
Saint-Charles de Potyze Cemetery
ZUIDERING
Menin Road Museum
Hell's Fire Corner
Hill 62/Sanctuary Wood
Hoge Voete
Zillebeke
Hagebos
Wieltje
MEENSEWEG Hoge
BRUSSEWEG
Sint-Jan
N332
N313
Polijze
Hoveland
Front Line April 1918
Bedford House Cemetery
Saint-Eloi Crater
Plickem
NOORDERING
Brieke
Ieper Town Cemetery
Front Line April 1918
N37
RIJSELSEWEG
N336
Ypres (Ieper)
Ramparts War Museum & Cemetery
OOSTKAAI
Essex Farm Cemetery
see inset
Ypres (Ieper)
N38
BARGIESTRAAT
Yser/Ieper Kanaal
Poperinge
N375
Ter Olmen
Wit Huis
Boezinge
Yorkshire Trench
N369
DIKSMUIDSEWEG
N8

His tale was true of many poor boys that lied about their age for the chance of regular meals, pay and clothes. You'll note that in many of the cemeteries you visit the spacing and orientation of the headstones change. This indicates that the cemetery sat close to, or on, the Front Line and rather than incorrectly marking the resting place of soldiers whose graves had been destroyed by artillery fire, gaps were left.

YORKSHIRE TRENCH (*Bargiestraat, behind industrial estate;* ⊕ *daily; free entry; W/A*) This British trench was discovered behind a Boezinge industrial estate in 1997 (see box, page 20) and dates from 1915. It was acquired by the In Flanders Fields Museum (see page 15), where you can see an exhibition of the objects they found.

SAINT-CHARLES DE POTYZE CEMETERY (*Zonnebeekseweg;* ⊕ *daily; free entry; W/A with help*) Situated 3km northeast of Ypres city centre, this cemetery was incredibly close to the Front Line. The remains of more than 4,000 French soldiers are interred here, as well as a further unidentified 600 souls buried in a mass grave.

HILL 60 (*Zwarteleenstraat 40, Zillebeke*) This manmade hillock – no higher than a second-floor window – was formed in the 1860s during the creation of the Ypres–Comines railway. The steam trains had struggled with the slight incline, so locals had flattened the land and dumped the leftover earth in a pile by the side of the tracks. Prior to the war, the grassy bump was known as Lovers' Knoll, popular with courting couples who came here for a cuddle while enjoying the views. But it was these views that made it the source of intense fighting between the Allied and German forces, and by 1915 it was one of the most feared places on the Front Line. Control of the hill passed back and forth between British and Germans with a series of suicidal attacks and counterattacks. The biggest breakthrough came on 7 June 1917, during the Battle of Messines (see box, page 29), when

Strudwick grave, Essex Farm Cemetery (ET)

British tunnellers detonated 53,000lbs of explosives under German lines – the resulting craters can still be seen today.

To get there troops had to march past **Hell's Fire Corner**, an infamous roundabout on the Menin Road where German artillery reached within one yard of the road. Several soldiers were killed here before even making it to the Front Line.

BEDFORD HOUSE CEMETERY (*2.5km south of Ypres along Rijselseweg, on left-hand side; free entry; W/A*) 'Bedford House' was the name Commonwealth soldiers gave to Chateau Rosendal, a moated country house set in woodland, that once stood here. It was used as a field station and as brigade headquarters, but eventually both the trees and house were destroyed by shellfire.

SAINT-ELOI CRATER (*Rijselseweg 214, access through a small green gate;* ⊕ *1 Apr–15 Nov 09.00–17.00; free entry*) This pretty reed-strewn pond is the largest of the craters created by the mines detonated during the Battle of Messines (see box, page 29). Nearby stands a British bunker.

MENIN ROAD MUSEUM (*Meenseweg 470, inside Café–Feestzaal Canada;* ☏ *057 20 11 36; www.meninroadmuseum.com;* ⊕ *10.00–22.00 Mon & Wed–Sun; adult/under 12s €3.50/free*) Small privately owned museum displaying original artefacts recovered from exposed trenches and dugouts.

BOEZINGE

Most people have heard of Passchendaele and Messines and the great battles associated with them, but few have heard of Boezinge – a small village north of Ypres on the banks of the Ieperlee Canal. In April 1915, during the Second Battle of Ypres, the German army was forcing French troops back across Pilkem Ridge. The French dug in just before reaching the canal and held the Allied Line until the British 4th Division relieved them in June. They began advancing across No Man's Land on 6 July 1915. They sustained heavy losses, but were able to push the Allied Line forward until it was less than 100 yards from the Germans. General Sir Herbert Plumer claimed 'the attack ... [was] one of the great battles of the campaign'.

When the war ended, the fighting ground was left fallow and forgotten until the late 1990s when a local volunteer group of archaeologists and historians called The Diggers obtained a permit to excavate. After digging barely 3ft they uncovered trenches, dugouts, thousands of artefacts and undetonated bombs (incredibly the Belgian Army still uncover 200 tonnes every year). Most poignantly, in 2002, behind the Boezinge Industrial Estate, they uncovered the remains of 205 British, German and French soldiers believed to have died in a gas attack. They lay hunched on the ground, still holding their guns and wearing their helmets. Sadly, any identifying markers such as dog tags or uniforms had long since rotted away and none could be identified. Their remains were reinterred in the surrounding cemeteries. The land will be built over soon to make way for the expansion of the estate, and if it hadn't been for The Diggers the efforts of the British 4th Division would have remained buried and forgotten.

German soldiers of the 238th Reserve Infantry Regiment mourning the death of a comrade. The second soldier from the right was killed in action two days after the photograph was taken (VDK)

SANCTUARY WOOD/HILL 62 (*Canadalaan 26, Zillebeke;* ☎ *057 46 63 73;* ⏰ *10.00–18.00 daily; adult/under 14s €8/5*) Superb privately owned museum that doesn't sanitise the war. The land belonged to a farmer, who left the British trench system and shell holes in place when he returned after the war. It's one of the last original trench systems to survive; most have been filled in. The museum rooms are bursting with accumulated rifles, shell casings, helmets and, best of all, stereoscopes containing original 3D war photographs – although be warned: some of them are quite graphic.

HOOGE CRATER MUSEUM (*Meenseweg 467, Zillebeke;* ☎ *057 46 84 46; www.hoogecrater.com;* ⏰ *10.00–18.00 Tue–Sat, 10.00–21.00 Sun, closed Jan; adult/child €4.50/2*) Housed in a 1920s chapel, this quaint two-room museum contains the private collection of curator Niek Bennot and his friend Phillipe Oosterlinck. They've amassed a good collection of clothing (displayed on mannequins), helmets, shells as well as a 1916 ambulance and a Fokker DR1 German warplane. The now-flooded Hooge Crater lies 100m east. It was created by the British during the Second Battle of Ypres when they smuggled 1,700kg of dynamite down specially built tunnels that ran under the German front line and detonated them on 19 July 1915 in an effort to break up the enemy's formation.

VANCOUVER CORNER (*Brugseweg & Zonnebekestraat crossroads, Poelkapelle; W/A with help*) This small garden is dominated by the statue of the **Brooding Soldier**. Carved from a single piece of solid granite it was erected in memory of the 1st Canadian Division who were wiped out by a gas attack on 24 April 1915. The ferns planted round about are meant to mimic the creeping green-tinted gas.

LANGEMARK GERMAN MILITARY CEMETERY (DEUTSCHER SOLDATENFRIEDHOF) (*Klerkenstraat; www.langemark-poelkapelle.be;* ⏰ *daily; free entry; W/A*) Dotted with oak trees – the national symbol of Germany – Langemark is one of four German cemeteries left in Flanders. Originally there were 68, but many were consolidated or the soldiers' remains were reinterred back home. Hitler visited the cemetery in June 1940 while Flanders was under German occupation following the Battle of France. Inside the entrance arch, carved into oak panels, are the names of the **Student Soldiers**: university students who volunteered to join the war, but were only given six weeks training before being sent to the Western Front – often to the worst parts.

On the other side of the gate sits a square mass grave containing the remains of 24,000 unknown soldiers and beyond this, at the back of the compound, the statue of the **Mourning Soldiers**: four slumped figures modelled on a 1918 photograph of the Reserve Infantry Regiment 238 mourning at the graveside of their comrade (see photo, above). The trios of basalt crosses dotted throughout the cemetery are purely for decoration.

The infamous Third Battle of Ypres – also known as the Battle of Passchendaele – was one of the bloodiest battles of World War I. In the summer of 1917, fighting on Germany's east border had stopped due to the Russian Revolution and it was possible to redeploy German troops west. Faced with this imminent surge in German military strength, Britain knew it had to act quickly. Sir Douglas Haig developed a plan whose main aims were to reclaim the high ground at Passchendaele and push the Germans back from the coast in order to destroy their submarine bases, which continually threatened Britain's supply lines and the American reinforcements arriving by ship. Buoyed by success at the Battle of Messines (see box, page 29) in June, the plan was given the go-ahead and to 'clear the way' for his troops Haig ordered a massive two-week bombardment. Then on 31 July 1917, Haig sent Allied troops over the top, but a few days later the heavens opened and the worst deluge to hit the region in 30 years turned Flanders' Fields into a quagmire. Tanks got stuck, gun mechanisms jammed and crater holes that used to provide shelter from enemy fire filled with water. Men and horses drowned in the worst sections. Haig called off the attack, but stubbornly issued another on the 16 August, others on 20 and 26 September, and another on 4 October. By the time Allied forces reached Passchendaele on 6 November, 325,000 Allied soldiers and 260,000 German troops had lost their lives for the sake of five miles of land. To give a sense of the scale of the loss, it is estimated that for every square metre gained, 435 men died. Aerial photographs of Passchendaele after the war show a pockmarked lunar expanse of complete devastation (see photo below).

In an attempt to gain an advantage before American troops arrived in Europe, the German army embarked on the Lys Offensive in April 1918 and in the space of three days pushed the Allies all the way back to the outskirts of Ypres, reoccupying the land taken by the Allies during the Third Battle of Ypres. However, the effort exhausted the final reserves of the German army and it was unable to resist the Allies' Hundred Days Offensive in August 1918. A few months later, on 11 November, the Armistice was signed in a railway carriage in Compiègne Forest, just north of Paris (see box, page 83).

Aerial photographs of Passchendaele taken before and after World War I (W)

GUYNEMER MONUMENT (*Guynemerplein, Poelkapelle; W/A*) This monument, which stands in the village of Poelkapelle northeast of Ypres, is dedicated to Georges Guynemer – a wartime French pilot. He belonged to an elite French Air Force corps called the Escadrille des Cigognes (Stork Squadron) and he succeeded in shooting down over 50 German fighter airplanes at a time when dogfighting tactics were still in their infancy.

Sadly, on 11 September 1917 Guynemer clambered aboard his Spad biplane for a reconnaissance mission over Ypres. He was never seen again and his body was never found. Rumours suggest he was shot down near Poelkapelle, but the land was too decimated by shelling to recover any evidence. As a nod to the name of his squadron, a bronze stork tops the monument; its wings pointing in the direction of where Guynemer is said to have crashed. Guynemer's last routine orders are carved into the stone.

ZONNEBEKE

MEMORIAL MUSEUM PASSCHENDAELE 1917 (*Ieperstraat* 7A; 051 77 04 41; *www. passchendaele.be;* 09.00–17.00 daily, closed 16 Dec–31 Jan; adult/under 12s €7.50/ free; not W/A) Inside Kasteel Zonnebeke, a 1920s mansion, this museum has been transformed in time for the centenary. In the old section is a collection of weaponry, uniforms and an immersive trench 'experience' complete with corrugated-iron walkways, bunker rooms, dim lights and war-sounds soundtrack.

The brand-new wing explains, via a large-scale model, the 100-day Battle of Passchendaele (see box, opposite) that claimed the lives of hundreds of thousands of soldiers in 1917, as well as how trench design developed over the years, with examples of how the German and British versions differed. The Remembrance Gallery houses a sculpture by New Zealand artist Helen Pollock – it's made from clay scraped from soil in Passchendaele and Coromandel (New Zealand).

Next door is the new Passchendaele Memorial Park with poppy gardens dedicated to the various nationalities that fought in the battle. From here you can walk the 3km (2 miles) to Tyne Cot Cemetery – they're developing a smartphone guide for the walk; ask at reception for details.

TYNE COT CEMETERY (*Vijfwegestraat 1;* 051 77 04 41; *www.passchendaele.be;* 1 Feb–30 Nov 10.00–18.00 daily; free entry; W/A with help) Tyne Cot is the world's largest Commonwealth war-grave cemetery and the final resting place for 11,954 souls. The sight of its uniform graves stretching into the distance is utterly humbling. Over 70% of them belong to unidentified British or Commonwealth soldiers and bear the words 'Known unto God'. The cemetery takes its name from a barn that once stood at the centre of this German strongpoint, and which British troops presumably thought resembled a Tyneside cottage. The Germans had a couple of blockhouses or 'pillboxes' here which they used as Advance Dressing Stations (ADS). Several have been preserved, including the one beneath the mighty

Brooding Soldier, Vancouver Corner (ET)

Memorial Museum Passchendaele 1917 (MMP/VF)

Cross of Sacrifice erected in 1922. Gently climb a few of its steps, and you get a glimpse of the Germans' advantageous viewpoint overlooking the British lines and Ypres. It was this high ground for which the British fought at the Third Battle of Ypres (see box, page 22).

POLYGON WOOD CEMETERY AND BUTTES NEW BRITISH CEMETERY (*Lange Dreve 5; ☉ daily; free entry; W/A*).

The small Polygon Wood Cemetery is named after a large wood that covered this area prior to the war. It passed back and forth during the fighting, but finally retaken by the 9th Scottish Division on 28 September 1918.

Walk across the road, via a walled avenue, past the Cross of Sacrifice, to the Buttes New British Cemetery. Ahead of you, on the hill, is the memorial to the 5th Australian Division, who captured the wood on 26 September 1917. The cemetery contains the graves of 2,108 Commonwealth servicemen, of which 1,677 are unidentified. Also standing here is the New Zealand Memorial – a mark of respect to the 378 officers who died here between September 1917 and May 1918 and have no known grave.

COMMAND BUNKER (*Komenstraat, Zandvoorde; ☉ daily; free entry*)

Preserved by the Memorial Museum Passchendaele 1917 (see page 23), this reinforced-concrete 19m-long German bunker was built in 1916 by the 3rd Company of Armierungsbatallion No 27 and used as a command post – look for the plaque they erected on the bunker wall saying so. At the time, it was situated just 6km from the Front Line. A series of six rooms can be explored.

Building of Tyne Cot Cemetery (MMP/VF)

4

Poperinge and Heuvelland

POPERINGE

Like Veurne (see page 32), Poperinge was one of the few towns to remain under Allied control throughout the war and didn't see fighting. As a result, it was a haven for soldiers travelling to and from the Front Line. Troops referred to it affectionately as 'Pops'. Talbot House, in particular, became a legendary place of respite where soldiers could take needed rest and let off steam. The compact town makes an excellent day trip from Ypres and shouldn't be missed.

GETTING THERE AND AWAY From Ypres **by car**, follow the N308 west (*13.5km; approx 20mins*). You can also get to Poperinge from Ypres **by train** (*21mins past the hour Mon–Fri, 22mins past the hour Sat–Sun; 7mins*).

WHAT TO SEE AND DO
De Cellen (*Guido Gezellestraat;* ⏰ *06.00–22.00 daily; free entry; W/A*) Just around the corner from the Stadhuis and tucked away off the street, this courtyard is the site of a very dark chapter in British World War I history. British soldiers who refused to return to the Front Line or were caught deserting – often as a result of trauma – were held in these two cells and executed at the wooden post standing at the back of the courtyard. A priest would read them their last rights, the attending medical officer would place a white cloth over their heart and a line of six riflemen would face the accused, but only one of the guns was loaded.

Now a memorial, the cell walls have been covered with Perspex to protect the graffiti carved by soldiers awaiting execution. One such man was 31-year-old Eric Poole, a first officer who developed shellshock, but was sent back to the Front and arrested two days later when he tried to escape. He was executed here on 10 December 1916 at 07.25.

Talbot House (*Gasthuisstraat 43, entrance via Pottestraat;* 📞 *057 33 32 28; www. talbothouse.be;* ⏰ *10.00–17.30 Tue–Sun; adult/over 65s/7–22/under 7s €8/7/5/free, last ticket 16.30; not W/A*) Talbot House is a very special living museum that was established in December 1915 by the Reverend Philip Clayton – best known as 'Tubby' – and chaplain Neville Talbot as a bed and breakfast for soldiers travelling to and from the Front Line.

Originally from Queensland, Australia, Tubby was assigned to the 6th Division as an army chaplain and posted to the salient when World War I broke out. He visited the trenches, or 'slums' as he called them, several times and narrowly escaped death on a number of occasions. He saw firsthand the unspeakable horrors soldiers faced, so he and Talbot opened the bed and breakfast as a place of 'light, warmth and laughter', a shelter from the ugliness of war and named it after Neville's brother,

Talbot House, Chaplain's Room (ET)

Gilbert, who had died in combat. Here soldiers could make as much noise as they liked, play card games and have an undisturbed night's sleep. Indeed, the 'real sheets' room (The General's Room) was famous as the only room in the house with a bedsheet – a luxury which cost five francs and was the prize of many a card game. By the summer of 1917, it's estimated 5,000 soldiers a week were passing through the house in preparation for the Third Battle of Ypres (see box, page 22).

Tubby was a jovial landlord, famous for his love of humorous adages, such as 'Never judge a man by his umbrella, it might not be his', and several are pinned above the doorways. In the chapel, which sits on the fourth floor beneath the eaves, he baptised 50 soldiers, performed 800 confirmations and delivered communion to tens of thousands of soldiers.

The house is filled with original items, but the two most poignant artefacts are found in the hallway on the ground floor. The first is 'Friendship corner', a yellowing typed-out list from the visitors' book where soldiers would leave messages for

TOURIST INFORMATION

Toerisme Poperinge Grote Markt 1; ✎ 057 34 66 76; www.toerismepoperinge.be; ⏱ 1 Apr–30 Sep 09.00–12.00 & 13.00–17.00 Mon–Fri, 09.00–12.00 & 13.00–16.00 Sat–Sun; 1 Oct–31 Mar 09.00–12.00 & 13.00–17.00 Mon–Fri, 09.00–12.00 & 13.00–16.00 Sat. Narrow office in the Stadhuis basement. They sell a 34km *POProute* cycling map, which takes you past the cemeteries.

friends, or notes asking others if they knew of their whereabouts. The second, by the original entrance, is a map of the Ypres Salient (currently a photocopy; the original is undergoing restoration). Poperinge and Ypres have been wiped away by the fingerprints of soldiers pointing to where they were stationed or had lost friends – you can even make out the smudgy bulge of the salient.

After the war, Tubby was made an honorary citizen of Poperinge. He returned to England in March 1919, accompanied by his dog Chippy, and became the vicar of All Hallows Church near the Tower of London.

Talbot House was, and will remain, a hugely important place of remembrance for World War I veterans, like Harry Patch – the last surviving soldier to have fought in the trenches during World War I – who visited the house before his death in 2009 and was able to sit in the same lounge chair he'd last sat in while talking to friends in 1917.

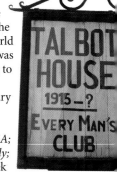

Afterwards, volunteers are happy to make you a complimentary cup of tea or coffee in the kitchen.

Lijssenthoek Military Cemetery (*Boescheepseweg 35A;* ✎ *057 34 66 76; www.lijssenthoek.be;* ⏱ *09.00–18.00 daily; free entry; W/A*) About 1½ miles west of Poperinge, Lijssenthoek is the second-largest Commonwealth cemetery in the world, after Tyne Cot (see page 23) with 10,784 graves. Over 8,000 of

Talbot House sign, Poperinge (ET)

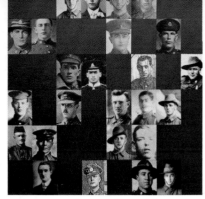

Faces of the Fallen, Lijssenthoek Cemetery (VF)

these are white-sandstone British Army headstones, as well as 300 French white crosses and 130 German stones – the latter are fittingly placed under oak trees at the back. There is also a collection of Chinese graves on the far left-hand side.

From 1915 to 1920, it was known as Remy Siding and was the site of the biggest field hospital in the Ypres Salient. The new low-lying information centre contains excellent information panels about the hospital, as well as databanks to search for relatives and listening points on a red wall that issue snippets of soldiers' stories.

HEUVELLAND

Unlike nearby Poperinge, this rural stretch of land south of Ypres was overrun with fighting during World War I. Opposing forces clamoured to claim the region's hills that provided observation points and views over the enemy. Many of the villages were flattened and the surrounding fields still bear the pockmarks and craters of heavy fire.

GETTING THERE AND AWAY Heuvelland is very rural and best explored **by car** or **by bike**. The tourist information office can help you arrange the latter (see page opposite). From Ypres station take **bus** No 70 (direction Nieuwkerke) to Kemmel; journey time 26 minutes; a day pass €5 (€7 if bought on board).

WHAT TO SEE AND DO
Kemmel This is the area's most central village with the best tourist information centre (see page 28). From here, you can organise bike, walking or guided tours to see the other sites in the region.

'Den Engel' Monument aux Soldats Francais (French Soldier Memorial)
(*Kemmelberg; W/A with help*) This towering 18m-high column with an angel relief stands atop Kemmelberg – a famous hill that was fought over between the French and Germans during the Battle of Lys in April 1918 because it offered extensive views towards Mesen (Messines) and Ypres (Ieper). The angel overlooks the battlefield and, lower down the slope, is an ossuary (mass grave) containing the remains of the 5,000 French soldiers who died trying to defend the elevated site.

Lettenberg Bunkers (*Lokerstraat; ⊕ 09.00–18.00 daily; free entry*) The British built these underground command posts and sleeping quarters – situated on the other side of the hill from the 'Den Engel' monument – while the Allies had control of Kemmelberg hill. The wooden sleeping compartments collapsed, but you can still visit the reinforced-concrete bunkers.

WORLD WAR I PHONE APP

Free downloads are available at www.1418remembered.co.uk. Download from the Apple app store and Google Play.

Wijtschate This tiny village lies just 3km to the east of Kemmel and can be easily reached on foot or by bike.

Bayernwald (*Voormezelestraat;* ⏰ *10.00–18.00 daily; €4/1 adult/child, but tickets from Kemmel Tourist Office; W/A*) Roughly 1km north of Wijtschate, this elevated wooded ground 40 metres above sea level was won by the Germans after fierce fighting and was a key site during the Battle of Messines (see box, opposite). They developed an impregnable system of trenches, bunkers and mine shafts but today you can only see about ten per cent of what was there during the war. Nevertheless, it's chilling to walk the same pathways the soldiers followed.

'Pool of Peace' (Spanbroekmolen Mine Crater) (*Kruisstraat; free entry*) On 7 June 1917, the British army detonated 19 mines under German-held land between Hill 60 (see page 19) and Ploegsteert. The peaceful lily pad-covered pool you see today was one of the craters created by the explosions. It's over 12m deep and 129m diameter; it can be found between the villages of Kemmel and Wijtschate. Interestingly, it's privately owned by Talbot House in Poperinge (see page 25).

MESSINES (MESEN)

Belgium's smallest city offered crucial high ground and for the first three years of the war, the Germans held on to the Messines Ridge tightly. They lost control in June 1917 at the Battle of Messines (see box, opposite).

GETTING THERE AND AWAY From Ypres take **bus** No 72 (direction Le Bizet) to Messines; journey time 15 minutes; day pass €5.

WHAT TO SEE AND DO
Historical Museum (*Markt 1;* ☏ *057 44 50 41;* ⏰ *09.00–12.00 & 13.00–17.00 Mon–Fri, Easter–11 Nov also 14.30–17.30 Sun; admission €1.50*) Amid information on the town's medieval history are World War I artefacts and memorabilia, as well as an explanation of the Battle of Messines (see box, opposite).

Pool of Peace, Wijschate (W/VF)

Irish Peace Park (Irish Peace Tower) (*Armentiersesteenweg;* ⊕ *09.00–17.00 Mon–Fri; guided tours possible, ask tourist office; free entry; W/A*) Just south of Messines village centre, this memorial park is dedicated to all Irish soldiers killed or wounded during World War I. Its main feature is a 33m-high tower built in traditional 8th-century Irish style and made from stones reclaimed from a demolished workhouse in County Westmeath in Ireland. Amazingly, the inside of the tower only sees light on the 11th hour of the 11th day in November thanks to a trick of design.

Messines Ridge British Cemetery (*Nieuwkerkestraat;* ⊕ *daily; free entry; W/A*) When the Armistice was signed, graves from numerous impromptu burial plots in the surrounding area were moved here for proper interment. Today, there are 1,534 Commonwealth graves, of which 957 are unidentified.

At the entrance is the Messines Ridge New Zealand Memorial to the Missing, carved with the names of 839 soldiers who died in the Battle of Messines (see box, below) and have no known grave.

BATTLE OF MESSINES

The aim of this week-long attack, 7–14 June 1917, was to overwhelm German defences and capture the Messines Ridge, a key section of high ground that overlooked the fields south of Ypres. British General Herbert Plumer had been preparing for the attack 18 months in advance. 'Sappers' had been digging tunnels that stretched under German lines and, at times, they'd meet counter-tunnellers digging towards British lines – hand-to-hand combat would breakout underground.

Twenty-two mines – over 600 tonnes of explosives – were placed at the end of the shafts and on the eve of the attack Plumer said the following to his staff: 'Gentlemen, we may not make history tomorrow, but we shall certainly change the geography.' At 03.10 that morning, 19 of the mines safely detonated and the German line was blown to smithereens – over 10,000 soldiers were killed outright. It's rumoured the explosion was so loud it was heard by war-cabinet minister Lloyd George in Downing Street, London.

Allied troops advanced, keeping up a barrage of gunfire, and within hours British and New Zealand troops had conquered the ridge. The battle is considered one of the biggest successes of the Allied Forces, but it was the precursor to the larger and bloodier Third Battle of Ypres (see box, page 22).

Diksmuide, Veurne and Nieuwpoort

DIKSMUIDE

Wandering around Diksmuide's pleasant Grote Markt listening to the golden-oldie tunes being softly piped out across the square, it's hard to imagine the intense conflicts played out here during World War I. From the very start, the town became embroiled in the Battle of Yser, which effectively dismantled Germany's Schlieffen Plan and established the boundaries of the Front Line that would barely move for the next four years.

The main sites of interest are the IJzer Tower peace monument and the preserved Dodengang trenches, but do take the time to buy a couple of *Ijzerbollen* – local custard-filled creations.

GETTING THERE AND AWAY

By car From Ypres follow the N369 north (*22.6km; approx 30mins*); from Veurne follow the N36 westwards (*17.4km; approx 20mins*); from Brugge follow the N31 south and merge with the E40 (direction Oostende), take exit 4 (direction Middelkerke) and follow the N369 south (*50km; approx 47mins*).

By train Ypres via Kortrijk and Lichtervelde (*39mins past the hour daily; 2hrs 11mins*); Bruges via Lichtervelde (*7mins past the hour daily; 43mins*); Ghent (*51mins past the hour daily; 59mins*); Veurne (*3mins past the hour daily; 11mins*).

GUIDED TOURS

Helipromotions 51 50 56 56; www.battlefields.be. Offers 30, 45 & 60min battlefield tours by helicopter. Starts from the heliport in Diksmuide & flies over the Westhoek. Prices start at €295.
Rent A Guide 0488 40 74 40; www.rentaguide.be. Offers 3hr minibus tours of IJzer Front starting at 09.30 & returning by

14.00; €30 per person. Departs from Diksmuide's Grote Markt & takes in Vladslo, Dodengang & Nieuwpoort.
Scooterzone Kleine Dries 29b; 51 50 57 29; www.scooterzone.be. Rent 2-seater scooters equipped with a GPS unit programmed with World War I sites.

IJzer Tower, Diksmuide (W/V)

WHAT TO SEE AND DO

IJzer Tower (IJzertoren) (*Ijzerdijk 49;* 051 50 02 86; www.ijzertoren.org; ⏱ *Oct–Mar 09.00–17.00 Mon–Fri, 10.00–17.00 Sat–Sun; Apr–Sep 09.00–18.00 Mon–Fri, 10.00–18.00 Sat–Sun; adult/over 65s/7–25/under 6s €7/5/1/free; W/A with help, some floors off-limits*) The cross-shaped IJzer Tower protrudes 84m above the horizon; a giant, and defiant, monument to peace. Erected in 1965, its base is inscribed with

Diksmuide Tourist Office Grote Markt 28; ☎ 051 79 30 50; www.toerisme.diksmuide.be; ⏱ 1 Apr–15 Nov 10.00–12.00 & 14.00–17.00 daily; 16 Nov–30 Mar 10.00–12.00 & 14.00–17.00 Mon–Fri. Sells the *IJzer Front* 79km car route map in English, which takes you on a tour of the sites & memorials associated with the Battle of Yser (see box, page 34). They also sell the *Nooit meer Oorlog* cycling map (37.5km), which takes you past Vladslo Cemetery, the trenches & IJzer Tower. They can also arrange guided tours (€50/2hrs).

the words 'No More War' in four languages and its 22 levels are dedicated to the retelling of the war (and a bit on Belgian politics too). Starting at the very top of the tower, which offers sweeping 360° views of the landscape, you work your way down, experiencing dim and frightening recreated trenches (level 3), and the smell of mustard and chlorine gas (level 15).

Prior to entering the tower, you buy your tickets from the 1960s building on the right, just after the bridge. You exit out the back of the building and you have to walk through a replica trench – complete with sandbags and smoke machines – and across a duck pond with bomb sound effects timed with splashes in water, so it feels like you're under attack. This route leads you to the **PAX gate**, a monumental archway built in 1950 from the ruined remains of the first IJzer Tower which was built in 1928 but blown up on 15 March 1946 by pro-French Belgian military members who opposed the growing strength of the Flemish Independence Movement. The tower was a target because it contains the graves of eight leading Flemish freedom fighters.

Passing by the gate, you enter a compound where the first tower stood – button #4 on the right-hand wall gives an explanation of its various elements in English. What's most important to notice is the inscription on the eight freedom-fighters' graves: AVV, VVK 'Alles voor Vlaanderen, Vlaanderen voor Kristus' (All for Flanders, Flanders for Christ). Prior to World War I, the Flemish were at a distinct

'The Grieving Parents', Vladslo Cemetery
(HK/VF)

social disadvantage to their French-speaking Wallonian countrymen: there were no Flemish schools, and if you couldn't speak French you couldn't qualify as an officer. The discrepancies angered Flemish soldiers, who began to question why they should fight and die for their country when the government would place a tombstone bearing a French motto on their grave. The Flemish Independence Movement came up with the above.

Dodengang (*Ijzerdijk 65;* \ *051 50 33 44;* ⊕ *1 Apr–15 Nov 10.00–17.00 daily; 16 Nov–31 Mar 09.30–16.00 Tue & Fri; free entry; W/A with help*) Located 2km north of the IJzer Tower, this 400m stretch of preserved trenches has been carefully maintained 'Lest we forget'. Allied troops called it the Trench of Death and spent four years here bravely holding the Front Line.

Vladslo War Cemetery (*Houtlandstraat 3, 8600 Vladso-Diksmuide;* ⊕ *daily; free entry*) Over 25,000 soldiers are buried at this German war cemetery, which also contains the hugely moving *Grieving Parents* sculpture created by Käthe Kollwitz whose 18-year-old son, Peter, was killed in the war.

To get there you can cycle or call the Belbus (\ *059 56 52 56*) two hours prior to the time you want to travel. It'll pick you up from an agreed spot and drop you on Houtlandstraat, a 400m walk from the cemetery. Alternatively you can call a taxi (\ *0498 39 96 99*).

VEURNE

Just four miles from the French border and the North Sea coastline, Veurne – or Furnes as its known in French – boasts one of Flanders's most authentic market squares because the town was situated 9km from the Front Line during World War I and, as a result, many of its 16th-century buildings avoided destruction.

GETTING THERE AND AWAY From Ypres **by car**, follow the N8 northwest (*31km; approx 35mins*). From Bruges R30 follow signs for the E40 and follow it west for 33.5km, then take exit 1a (*54km; approx 42mins*). If travelling **by train**, Bruges via Lichtervelde (*7mins past the hour daily; 54mins*); Ypres–Kortrijk–Lichtervelde–Veurne (*39mins past the hour daily; 2hrs 20mins*).

GETTING AROUND
Motorcenter Westhoek Vaartstraat 23; 058 31 14 46; www.motorcenterwesthoek.be. Rents 1 or 2-seater scooters & you can also follow a fixed World War I route using the GPS provided.

WHAT TO SEE AND DO
Stadhuis (Town Hall) (*Grote Markt 27;* ⊕ *tours: 1 Apr–15 Nov 10.00, 11.00, 14.00, 15.00 & 16.00 daily; 16 Nov–30 Mar 15.00 daily; €3; W/A ground floor only*) A pretty little thing tucked away in the western corner of the Grote Markt, it consists of two parts: the Stadhuis – easily recognisable thanks to its colonnade decorated with golden angels on a blue background – and the adjacent Landhuis. Unusually, the Stadhuis, which dates from 1596 (left side) and 1612 (right side), played second fiddle to the Renaissance-style Landhuis, serving as a hotel of sorts for officials attending meetings in the Landhuis. They were merged at the end of the French Revolution and served as headquarters of the Belgian Army during World War I when they narrowly avoided destruction – a series of photos in the Mayor's Cabinet shows how the bombs destroyed the row of four houses of the square and came within mere metres of the Landhuis.

The most elaborate of all the Stadhuis rooms is the Albert Hall, which King Albert I used as an office during World War I and where he met Britain's King George V. Beside the fireplace stands a portrait of local hero Karel Cogge (see box, page 34).

NIEUWPOORT

This chic coastal town was embroiled in the Battle of the Yser – part of the First Battle of Ypres – when its dam gates were opened to flood the Flemish plains and halt the German advancement.

GETTING THERE AND AWAY If travelling by **train** or **tram**, travel first to Ostende via Roeslaere (*1hr30mins*), then catch De Kust tram (*www.delijn.be/dekusttram/*) west to Nieuwpoort (*20mins*).

WHAT TO SEE AND DO
Ganzepoot Dam ('Goose Foot' Lock Complex) (*Kustweg;* 058 22 44 22; www. nieuwpoort.be; ⊕ *10.00–17.00 daily; adult/over 65s/child/under 12s €5/4/3/1*) The IJzer River reaches the sea at Nieuwpoort via this complex of locks. In 1914, an idea was hatched to open the sluices and flood the IJzer Plain to prevent the German advancement towards French ports and British supply lines – and it worked (see box, page 34). A new visitor centre describing the deliberate flooding will open in time for the centenary celebrations at the King Albert I Monument (see below).

King Albert I Monument (*Kustweg*) This circular, colonnaded monument was built in 1938 in honour of the king, who commanded the Belgian Army throughout the war. It's possible to walk around the top of the monument and survey the views over the IJzer Plain.

Ramskapelle Belgian Military Cemetery (*Ramskapellestraat 38, at the crossroads of the N367, running east from Nieuwpoort, & the N356;* ⊕ *daily; free entry*) This cemetery contains the graves of 635 Belgian soldiers, of which 400 are unidentified. The majority died in the 1914 Battle of Yser.

Intent on completing the first phase of the Schlieffen Plan – to capture Paris – the German Army advanced rapidly towards the Belgian coastline during the first few months of World War I. To halt their advance, Belgian troops established a Front Line 22 miles behind the Yser Canal, which ran from Nieuwpoort to Arras in France. However, during the Battle of Yser the Germans crossed the water and it was feared the Allies were on the verge of losing their hold in Belgium. (The tourist office publishes a car route map that takes you past monuments and memorials associated with the battle; see box, page 31).

Karel Cogge, a Veurne local and superintendent of the Northern Waterways, suggested they open the sluice gates at Nieuwpoort (see page 33) and slowly flood the area to halt the Germans. The idea was approved and on the 26 and 29 October 1914 the gates were raised, creating a marshland which spread as far as Diksmuide and was over a mile wide. Cogge's plan had single-handedly prevented Belgium becoming fully occupied and ended the German's 'Race to the Sea' for control of Calais and Dunkerque. In recognition of his services, Cogge was knighted in the Landhuis by King Albert I. Two paintings of him can be found in the Mayor's Cabinet of the Stadhuis and the Albert Hall of the Landhuis. His bust stands on Noordstraat.

King Albert I Memorial, Nieuwpoort (MPP/VF)

6

Mons

MONS

The elegant town of Mons lies in the French-speaking region of Wallonia, about 65km southwest of Brussels, and is best remembered for the Battle of Mons (see box, below). The city was captured almost immediately by the Germans and remained under their control until the Canadians liberated it on 11 November 1918. Poignantly, it was here that the first and last British soldiers died during World War I – you can see their graves at Saint-Symphorien Cemetary (see page 37).

TOURIST INFORMATION

Mons Tourist Office Grand Place 22; ☎ 065 33 55 80; www.visitmons.be; ⊕ 10.00–18.00 Mon–Sat & 11.00–17.00 Sun

GETTING THERE AND AWAY If you're staying in Ypres, drive **by car** southeast following the A19 towards Kortrijk, taking the E403 south to Tournai, picking up the E42 and then the E19 to Mons (*109km; approx 1hr*). **Trains** depart daily every half an hour from Ypres with a change at Bruxelles-Zuid/Gare-du-Midi (*1hr10mins; €31.60 return*).

THE BATTLE OF MONS

The Battle of Mons was the British Expeditionary Forces' (BEF) first engagement of World War I. The German army had been advancing across the Franco-Belgian border on its first stages of the Schlieffen Plan and on 23 August 1914 the British stepped in to block the outermost wing that threatened to encircle the Allies (particularly the French). Short on time, 80,000 BEF soldiers went up against 160,000 Germans, who also had twice the number of guns (600). Despite this, the BEF made a promising start: they hounded the Germans with rifle fire so intense and consistent the Germans believed they were using machine guns. There were numerous instances of bravery, including that of Lieutenant Maurice James Dease and Private Sydney Frank Godley (see page 37). However, by 15.00 that day British troops were ordered to retreat to the south of Mons and eventually they, and the French, were pushed back for the next two weeks.

Nevertheless, the battle was hailed as a success in Britain. Troops had been outnumbered three to one yet inflicted many more casualties than they sustained and they were able to escape. They'd also succeeded in protecting the French from being outflanked and delayed the Germans for a crucial 48 hours – not bad for an army that hadn't seen action since the Crimean War over 60 years before!

WHAT TO SEE AND DO

Memorial plaques, Town Hall (*Grand Place 22*) Happily, Mons' Gothic Town Hall escaped destruction during the war. You can only visit the interior by prior appointment (consult the tourist office; see page 35), but the feature of most interest is mounted on the exterior walls. Beside the entrance are two bronze plaques: one is dedicated to the 5th Royal Irish Lancers who took part in the two battles of Mons in 1914 and 1918; the other is dedicated to the 3rd Canadian Division that took part in the liberation fighting in November 1918.

Mons Cemetery (*Chemin de la Procession; take N6 north towards Brussels & after 600m turn right onto Chemin de la Procession, the cemetery is 1km on the left;* ⊕ *09.00–16.00 daily; free entry; W/A*) The communal cemetery was extended by the Germans and is now part of the town cemetery. Commonwealth, German, as well as Belgian, French, Italian, Russian and Romanian soldiers are buried here.

Saint-Symphorien Cemetery (Cimitière Saint-Symphorien) (*Rue Nestor Dehon; follow N90 2km east of Mons towards Charleroi, turn right off N90 onto N564 & Rue Nestor Dehon; the cemetery lies 200m along on the right-hand side; free entry*) Praised as the most beautiful on the Western Front, this leafy cemetery contains an equal number of German and British graves of soldiers killed in action during the battles of Mons; many belonged to the 4th Battalion of the Middlesex Regiment. There are a few notable graves to look out for: that of Private John Parr, the first British soldier to die in the conflict. On 21 August 1914, Parr's battalion sent him on a bicycle patrol near Casteau-Maisieres and their group was surprised by a German patrol and 20 year-old Parr was hit by gunfire. Private George Ellison of the 5th Irish Lancers was killed on 11 November 1918 and was the last casualty of the war. Also look out for Lieutenant Maurice James Dease (see below) who won the Victoria Cross for his bravery during the Battle of Mons.

Memorial to the first and last battles (*On the N90 & N40 crossroads*) East of town, this twin-pillar memorial stands in honour of those who fought in the first Battle of Mons in 1914 and the Canadian regiments who fought for 60 hours non-stop to reclaim the city in November 1918.

Irish Monument (*On the N90 & N40 crossroads*) Just across the road from the first-and-last battles memorial listed above, this Celtic cross honours the Royal Irish Rifles who fell at the First Battle of Mons.

Canal Bridge (*N6 towards Nimy & Brussels, Rue de Viaduc/Avenue de la Joyeuse Entrée*) If you drive, or walk, north of city you'll cross the Canal du Centre. Standing

on this bridge, you're overlooking salient ground – the British dug in one side, Germans on the other. Looking upstream you'll see an old railway bridge in the distance. It was this bridge that Lieutenant Maurice James Dease and Private Sydney Frank Godley, of the 4th Royal Fusiliers, defended with machine guns. Twenty four year-old Dease was shot five times and died in the ambulance on the way to a dressing station; Godley took over the gun and dismantled it before he was captured by the Germans. Godley survived and died shortly after World War II. Both were awarded the Victoria Cross for their bravery.

Centre: *Grave of Private John Parr – the first British soldier killed in World War I (WBT-JPR)*

Inset: *Grave of Private George Ellison – the last British soldier killed in World War I (WBT-JPR)*

THE ANGELS OF MONS

Legend has it that on the night of 23 August 1914, during the Battle of Mons, the British 7th Bremen Regiment, who had held Spiennes, found themselves almost encircled by German forces and annihilation seemed certain. However, as midnight struck, angel archers descended from the sky and held off the Germans, allowing the British to escape under the cover of darkness.

For years, conspiracy theories abounded as to whether this story was true. In fact, Welsh journalist and author Arthur Machen created the legend. He had heard reports of the fighting at the first Battle of Mons and how German troops had far outnumbered the British and realised how similar it was to the tale of phantom bowmen saving soldiers in the Battle of Agincourt. He submitted the piece as a short story, but his editor at *The Evening News* unintentionally ran it as a proper news feature because, up until then, Machen had written a number of factual pieces about the war.

The Angels of Mons *by Marcell Gillis (1934) (CVM)*

Part Three

FRANCE

BELGIUM

Aalst
A10
N6
Herzele
Aalst
N42
Silly
Soignies
N8
Ath
Beloeil
N7
E429
N60
Avelgem
N48
Rumes
N50
Mons
Feignies
Maubeuge
N2
Solre-le-
Château
Hautmont
Jeumont
Tielt
E17
A17
Tournai
D169
Bernissart
E19
Le Quesnoy
D649
Ors
D934
**Bleached bone'
memorial**
Fourmies
N2
D1043
Catillon
Roeselare
**Kortrijk
(Courtrai)**
Hallun
Roubaix
**Site of war's
biggest spy network**
Anzin
Valenciennes
Douchy-les-
Mines
**Le Quesnoy
Fortress**
Caudry
Le Catelet
N43
Wervik
N58
**Memorials to Resistance
& carrier pigeons**
Orchies
A23
Cambrai
D643
D644
Roisel
Poperinge
Ypres (Ieper)
Bailleul
Lille
Ascq
Seclin Fort
Seclin
A21
Douai
'**Deborah'
tank**
Somme
N8
E42
Erquinghem-
Lys
Armentières
N41
Lens
D643
Bapaume
E15
E19
The Western Front
**Battle of Loos & site
of Rudyard Kipling's
son's death**
**Vimy
Canadian National
Memorial**
Albert
Loos-en-
Gohelle
7 6
4
Arras
Battle of Arras
D929
Béthune
5
Pas-en-
Artois
Lucheux
D916
St-Omer
Auchel
Arvin
St-Pol-sur-
Ternoise
Doullens
N25
D948
**Memorial to the
Royal Flying Corps**
Wormhout
D916
D642
D943
Aire-sur-la-Lys
E15
Fruges
D928
D925
A16
Longuenesse
Aa
Oisemont
E40
Calais
Sangatte
Channel
tunnel
Wissant
**Dover Patrol
Memorial**
Ambleteuse
Marquise
E402
N42
Montreuil-sur Mer
**General headquarters
of Field Marshal Haig**
Hesdin
D939
Vron
Authie
Rue
E402
Berck
Étaples-sur-Mer
D901
Boulogne-sur-Mer
Outreau
2 1
3
D300

FRANCE

Strait of Dover

N
Bradt

0   20km
0 10 miles

See pages 45–6, 54, 56, 60 and 61 for details.

☐ **Cemeteries**
1 Boulogne Eastern Cemetery
2 Wimereux Communal Cemetery
3 Etaples Military Cemetery
4 La Maison Blanche German War Cemetery
5 Fromelles cemeteries
6 Memorial to the Great War (opening 2014)
   & Cabaret-Rouge British Cemetery
7 Notre-Dame de Lorette Cemetery

Le Nord and Lille

LILLE

Initially, Lille – the capital of Le Nord region – tricked the Germans into accepting it as a neutral or 'open city' at the outset of the war. The Allies refrained from bombarding throughout the conflict. However, on 3 October 1914, with the opposing armies attempting to outflank each other in their 'race to the sea', the Germans destroyed an entire section when the French desperately tried to defend the city. Lille capitulated on 13 October and wasn't liberated by British troops until 17 October 1918. By then, the Germans had inflicted considerable damage to the industrial and transport infrastructure.

Only a few kilometres behind the Western Front, Lille proved an ideal base for the Allies to contact a **Resistance movement** – a renegade collection of businessmen and petty criminals, led by Eugène Jacquet – whose members did everything they could to make life for the Germans as difficult as possible. In March 1915, they managed to return a pilot, whose plane had been shot down, back to Britain and a few months later he flew over Lille dropping leaflets mocking Governor Von Heinrich. Sadly, shortly after, the network's 200 members were betrayed and arrested. Jacquet and his closest comrades were shot on 22 September 1915 and the others were either sent to prison or deported. It's just one example of the bravery exhibited by young men during World War I.

GETTING THERE AND AWAY If crossing **by car** via the ferry to Calais, take the A16 towards Dunkerque then the A25, signposted for Lille (*74km; 90mins*). The same applies if you're using the Eurotunnel, though the A26 is that much closer. From Ypres, join the N365 south, then join N58 towards Armentières, then A25/E42 towards Lille (*40km; 40mins*). Remember, Lille is Rijsel in Flemish and will change on the road signs. Select Eurostar **trains** stop at Lille *en route* to Brussels.

TOURIST INFORMATION

Lille Tourist Office Palais Rihour, Pl Rihour; ☏ 03 59 57 94 00; e contact@lilletourism.com; www.lilletourism.com; ⏰ 09.00–18.00 Mon–Sat, 10.00–12.00 & 14.00–17.00 Sun & public holidays

WHAT TO SEE AND DO Lille's imposing **war memorial** on Place Rihour is built on the site of the old City Hall, which burnt down in 1916. Its post-war design is comprised of allegories: one evokes the fate of 30 hostages, who in July 1915 were held to coerce the townsfolk into working for the occupying army; a further 131 were deported in November 1916.

At the top of Boulevard Carnot, on the road to the Greater Lille towns of Roubaix and Tourcoing, a statue depicts a soldier kissing the hand of **Louise de Bettignies** – boss of probably the biggest spy network of the Great War (see box, page 43).

Roubaix suffered terribly under the Germans, who remained there from 14 October 1914 to 17 October 1918. It was only thanks to Dutch and American philanthropists that the industrial town, which relied heavily on imported resources, averted famine. A strong Resistance produced *L'Oiseau de France,* a newspaper containing reports from France and England, but the paper was shut down following a flurry of arrests in 1916.

Monument of Louise de Bettignies, Lille (V)

SECLIN

Seclin is a town with Gallo-Roman roots, situated 10km south of Lille. Like Lille, it was occupied by the Germans during the war.

GETTING THERE AND AWAY From Lille **by car**, follow the D549 south direct to Seclin (*10.2km; approx 21mins*). You can also get here **by train**. Trains depart Lille Flandres every 30 minutes (*12mins*).

TOURIST INFORMATION

Seclin Tourist Office 70 Rue Roger Bouvry; ☎ 03 20 90 12 12; www.seclin-tourisme.fr; ☾ 14.00–17.30 Mon, 09.00–12.30 & 14.00–17.30 Tue–Fri, 09.00–12.30 Sun

WHAT TO SEE AND DO

Fort de Seclin (*Chemin du Fort;* ☎ *03 20 97 14 18; www.fortseclin.com;* ☾ *from 15.00 Sat–Sun, closed early Nov–Easter weekend; adult/child €5/4; call or email for guided tour in English*). The Fort de Seclin was built in 1874 and was originally meant to join a line of 400 planned forts stretching from Nice to Dunkerque and between the North Sea and the Swiss border. It became part of Lille's 21 military posts. It didn't see much action, although a regiment of soldiers from the German state of Bavaria, stationed at the occupied fort, did take part in the Battle of Fromelles in July 1916 (see page 44). It was liberated in October 1918 by the British 6th Battalion The King's Liverpool Regiment and used as a field hospital until 1920.

Happily, father of five Didier Boniface then bought the abandoned fort in 1995 for one franc (!) and filled it with his carefully accumulated collection of military uniforms, medals, 'képis' and other peaked caps, German, French and British wagons, tanks and artillery, including the famous 13-pounder quick-firing field gun which was standard equipment for the British Royal Horse Artillery at the

LOCAL TOUCH

Fancy a tour by a local volunteer? Check out **Greeters** (*www.tourisme-nord.com*), part of a worldwide network of locals who volunteer to show you around their hometown for free.

outbreak of World War I. It now houses the 14–18 Museum and the family are busily converting the former Officers' Barracks into visitor accommodation.

Every year in mid October, the Fort celebrates its liberation by an English regiment with a reenactment day called the Journée du Poilu. Over the weekend, visitors can visit the museum and gain insight into camp life and gun shooting.

To get to Fort de Seclin **by car**, turn off the A1 Lille–Paris at junction 19.

ARMENTIÈRES

Sometimes nicknamed 'The Nursery' given its gentle surroundings, Armentières became, for the British during World War I, one of the best-known towns on the Western Front, made famous by a caustic British song entitled 'Mademoiselle from Armentières'.

GETTING THERE AND AWAY
From Lille **by car**, take the A25/E42 west towards Dunkerque and turn off at the junction with the D945 and follow the signs for Armentières (*20km; approx 25mins*). **Trains** depart from Lille Flandres direct to Armentières (*15mins*).

WHAT TO SEE AND DO
Cité Bonjean Cemetery (*Ave Roger Salengro, just off D945 before entering Erquinghem-Lys*) This vast expanse of headstones is the final resting place of 2,643 soldiers of various nationalities. The cemetery was opened in 1914 and then

Fort de Seclin (LNT)

used as a civilian cemetery because the one in nearby Bizet was too exposed to bombardment. The Cité Bonjean New Zealand Memorial is just one of the seven memorials in France and Belgium built in memory of the New Zealanders who fell on the Western Front.

Erquinghem-Lys Situated just a few kilometres from the Front, Erquinghem-Lys was for most of the war a forward base occupied by Commonwealth troops. However, in April 1918 the town was razed to the ground during a final attempt by the Germans to reach the North Sea. The **Churchyard Military Cemetery** contains 558 Commonwealth burials (eight of them unidentified) and 130 German burials. One unidentified Russian serviceman is also buried in the extension.

The stories of some of these soldiers have been brought to life by 60-year-old local historian and 'greeter' Michel Lannoo, who has set up a website covering the town's history (*www.erquinghem-lys.com; French only*) and containing recorded chats with British visitors who came to the Churchyard Military Cemetery and the separate **Suffolk Military Cemetery** (see box, opposite). Helping him is Jack Thorpe, whose Grimsby-born father was a British soldier who stayed on in France at the end of World War II for 'reasons of the heart'.

They have handed over their collection of medals, notebooks, paintings and other wartime items to the **Musée d'Ercan** (*Pl de l'Église;* 06 88 73 90 30; 14.30–18.00 *Sun, closed mid Nov–28 Feb; free entry*). Run by the local history association, it was built to commemorate a Front Line attack in 1917 – dubbed 'Dicky's Dash' – by a company of the Liverpool Scottish led by Captain Alan Dickinson MC.

The village of Erquinghem-Lys is a ten-minute drive southwest of Armentières along the D945. While you can get from Lille to Armentières by métro and bus (métro line 2 to St-Philibert, then bus No 77 or 79), it is quicker to take the TER train and then catch a taxi from Armentières to Erquinghem-Lys.

FROMELLES

Situated some 16km west of Lille, the village of Fromelles became the scene of bitter fighting in 1916 when the British High Command launched a major diversionary offensive on the village, which sat behind German lines, to prevent the Germans moving troops to the Battle of the Somme (see box, page 66).

In July 1916, the offensive deteriorated into the bloody **Battle of Fromelles**, which took place in open fields just northwest of the village. In just one night of fighting, the Australians sustained 5,533 casualties in what is described as the

In 1916, the Reverend David Railton, a locally based chaplain, visited the Churchyard and Suffolk military cemeteries at La Rolanderie Farm and saw the epitaph 'A Soldier of the Great War/Known unto God' carved on crosses. He vowed to provide a less stark way of honouring the dead once the fighting was over.

His promise was fulfilled in 1920 when, as part of British commemorations, one of six bodies exhumed from major battle areas on the Western Front was taken to Westminster Abbey on 11 November and interred in what became known as the Tomb of the Unknown Warrior. It is now one of the most visited war graves in the world and thereafter the idea of a symbolic tomb quickly spread worldwide. In France, La Tombe du Soldat Inconnu was placed in the Arc de Triomphe in Paris on 11 November 1920 as well.

worst 24 hours in the military history of their country. The British counted 1,547 casualties – dead, wounded or captured – and approximately 1,600 injured or dead German soldiers were also recorded. Many were teenagers, in what was probably a fruitless exercise because archive material strongly suggests the Germans already knew the attack was a ruse to divert attention from the Somme.

GETTING THERE AND AWAY Car is the only logical way to reach this small commune. Take the A25/E42 west out of Lille (towards Dunkerque), branch left onto the N41 (towards La Bassée), then first right onto D141 (*17.2km; approx 20mins*). Alternatively, arrange a guided tour through the Lille Tourist Office (see page 41).

WHAT TO SEE AND DO
VC Corner Australian Cemetery (*Rue Delval, on the D22C, 2km northwest of Fromelles on the road to Sailly-sur-la-Lys*) This is the only cemetery on the Western Front dedicated exclusively to Australian soldiers.

It consists of two mass graves covered with immaculate lawns and marked with a cross. The graves contain the remains of more than 400 Australian soldiers who were killed in the Battle of Fromelles on 19 July 1916. At the back of the plot stands

In 2007, passionate local historian Jean-Marie Bailleul realised, after researching German archives, that two mass graves were buried close to Pheasant Wood. He contacted Australian historians, who subsequently claimed the discovery as their own. In 2009, the graves were exhumed and DNA testing on buckles, buttons, press-studs and fragments of fabric enabled 250 of the bodies to be identified. Of these, 205 were Australians – of which 96 could be identified by name – and three were identified as British. In April 2013, a further five Aussie soldiers were identified and efforts to name more continue. Some of the bodies belonged to soldiers whose names are inscribed on the memorial wall. The remains of these individuals were transferred to the new Pheasant Wood Military Cemetery and reburied with named headstones.

A new free digital application is available to discover many unique sites of World War I including Fromelles (Le Nord), the Battle of Artois (Pas-de-Calais), Beaumont Hamel (The Somme), the Chemin des Dames (Aisne) and Lijssenthoek (Flanders). The programme is narrated by Guillaume Naylor, a 21st-century filmmaker out to rediscover World War I history. Download the 'Diaries 14–18' app directly from Apple's app store or the Google Play store or see the website http://bit.ly/diaries1418 for more details.

a memorial bearing the names of the 1,208 Australian soldiers who lost their lives in the offensive, but whose remains were never found.

Pheasant Wood Military Cemetery (*Rue de la Basse Ville opposite the St Jean-Baptiste Church*) This cemetery was created in January 2010 to welcome the bodies of 249 soldiers found in two mass graves by Pheasant Wood. On 19 July 2010, Prince Charles joined scores of relatives to mark its dedication and the burial – with full military honours – of the 250th soldier. The coffin was taken there by a military wagon drawn by horses from the King's Troop Royal Artillery. It is the first cemetery to be built by the Commonwealth War Graves Commission in 50 years.

Battle of Fromelles Museum (*no details yet released; contact Weppes tourist office*) This new museum is scheduled to open to visitors in Spring 2014, with an official opening in July. It replaces the eclectic collection originally displayed in Fromelles's town hall, which incidentally included a faded photo of a certain Adolf Hitler, then a 27-year-old corporal, who was rumoured to have been among the German ranks. He was a member of the 16th Bavarian Reserve Infantry Regiment, who fought in the battle.

Purposely half buried to represent the link between sky and earth, deceased soldiers and visitors, its octagonal centre will house an exhibition hall and the main focus will be the War Room, a circular space with a video presentation about the battle, as well as information on the various excavation works taking place.

Australian Memorial Park Located 200m down the road from the VC Memorial, this park opened in 1998 and features a **statue** entitled *Cobbers* which captures the Australian camaraderie and depicts Sergeant Simon Fraser, a farmer from Victoria, rescuing a fellow comrade from No Man's Land. The name is taken from a now-famous letter Fraser wrote a few days after the Battle of Fromelles:

'We found a fine haul of wounded and brought them in; but it was not where I heard this fellow calling, so I had another shot for it, and came across a splendid specimen of humanity trying to wriggle into a trench with a big wound in his thigh. He was about 14 stone weight, and I could not lift him on my back; but I managed to get him into an old trench, and told him to lie quiet while I got a stretcher. Then another man about 30 yards out sang out "Don't forget me, cobber". I went in and got four volunteers with stretchers, and we got both men in safely.'

'Cobbers' statue, Fromelles (LNT)

A TANK CALLED DEBORAH

Historian and hotelier Philippe Gorcynski is a man in love with a tank called Deborah. His persistence in rescuing the rusting World War I warrior from the battlefield mud around the village of Flesquières (11km from Cambrai off the E19/A2) in 1998 remains the stuff of local legend.

The tank is regarded as a historic monument and in November 2016 she will become the centrepiece of a **new museum** dedicated to the ferocious Battle of Cambrai (see page 48), in which the tank took part. 'Deborah' – officially known as tank Number D51 – was one of 476 employed by the British for the first time in 1917, appearing out of the November mist to cause confusion and considerable damage among the defending German forces. A vicious counterattack inevitably followed and tragically Deborah took a direct hit from five German shells which killed five of her eight-man crew. They were buried locally in the Flesquières Hill British Cemetery, but Deborah remained forgotten in the aftermath of the war.

That was until Philippe, frustrated for many years by rumours of a buried tank, began his mission both to find and save the rusting hulk. One villager, Madame Bouleux, reported that as a teenager she had seen prisoners being ordered by the Germans to push a tank into an enormous hole, but beyond this he had little to go on. It turns out his instincts – and Madame Bouleux's memory – were right. Six years later, after research visits to England's National Archives, the Tank Museum in Bovington and the Imperial War Museum in London, his dream of finding the precise location was fulfilled and on 5 November 1998, after digging for just one hour, the roof hatch was revealed.

By 20 November, the 81st anniversary of the Battle of Cambrai, the tank was fully exposed. A special ceremony, attracting worldwide interest, was held and a wreath laid in memory of the soldiers from the Tank Corps killed in the Battle of Cambrai. But the story doesn't end there. Thanks to the local association Tank de Flesquières (*www.tank-cambrai.com*), a monument was unveiled on the 90th anniversary of the battle. Dogged research has also revealed that the tank commander, 2nd Lieutenant Frank Heap, was awarded the Military Cross for leading some of his crew to safety. Many of his family members have visited Deborah, which now stands in a barn on a granite-cobble base made from some of the village's old streets.

'Deborah' excavated tank, Flesquieres (DG)

Walk An 8.5km signposted walk follows the footsteps of the Allied soldiers. Departing from Fromelles Church, the 2½ hour circuit takes a comprehensive look at ten major sites, with picnic areas and amenities along the way. Pick up a copy of the highly detailed and well-illustrated booklet from any local tourist office.

CAMBRAI

The areas around Cambrai were the location of two battles: the First Battle of Cambrai (20 November–3 December 1917), which involved the first successful use of tanks; and the Second Battle of Cambrai (8–10 October 1918).

TOURIST INFORMATION

Cambrai Tourist Office 48 Rue de Noyon; ☎ 03 27 78 36 15; www.tourisme-cambresis.fr; ⏱ 09.30–12.30 & 14.00–18.00 Mon–Sat, 14.30–17.30 Sun (closed Sun Nov–Mar)

GETTING THERE AND AWAY From Calais **by car**, follow the A26/E15 southeast, past Arras (*146km; approx 95mins*). Toll charge €7.20 each way. If arriving at Lille Europe via Eurostar, change to Lille Flandres for the regular direct trains to Cambrai, which can take up to an hour.

WHAT TO SEE AND DO
Cambrai Battlefield This site is one of the least visited on the Western Front; yet the November to December 1917 Battle of Cambrai was one of the bloodiest, and in the end pointless, offensives of the war. However, it was also the first battle where both sides applied tactical innovations that led to an end to the deadlock which had paralysed the war since 1914.

WILFRED OWEN

On 31 October 1918, in a forest close to the tiny village of Ors *(7km from Cateau-Cambresis off the D643 on the D959)*, one of Britain's greatest wartime poets, Wilfred Owen, scribbled his final letter to his mother by candlelight. Just days later, on 4 November, he was killed in a hail of machine-gun fire beside the Sambre-Oise Canal, a week before Armistice Day. He was just 25 years old.

Wilfred Owen grave, Ors (DG)

Owen, who had joined the Manchester Regiment as a private in his early twenties, was gassed during the Battle of the Somme and spent 28 hours holed up with the dismembered body of a fellow officer. When his nerves understandably snapped, doctors declared him unfit to command and he returned to the UK in June 1917 and spent a long spell in hospital near Edinburgh. During this time he collaborated with the celebrated anti-war poet Siegfried Sassoon producing such works of genius as *Anthem for Doomed Youth*, *Disabled*, and *Exposure*. He returned to the front in late August 1918.

British tanks were the most spectacular of these innovations (see box, page 47), used successfully on a large scale for the first time despite earlier disasters, such as their use at the Battle of the Somme in 1916 (see box, page 66). On 20 November the attack began along a 10km-wide front, with the Tank Corps providing 324 tanks, leading six infantry divisions. The bombardment took the Germans by surprise and, helped by shellfire, the tanks quickly reached the enemy trenches. Some 8,000 German prisoners were taken on the first day alone. By the evening, the British vanguard had gained 9km and was closing in.

But then it went badly wrong. Cavalry reinforcements, who were supposed to exploit the German disarray, were placed too far behind the lines. It took 15 hours to cover the final highly congested 5km to the Front.

The Germans rapidly reorganised and the push to Cambrai by British and Canadian forces was thwarted; by 29 November the enemy had sufficient reserves to counterattack. On 3 December, Haig gave orders to withdraw 'with the least possible delay.' All the ground gained in the initial stages had to be abandoned with high losses on both sides: 44,000 killed, wounded and lost in action on the Allied side and about 50,000 on the German side. But the trench stalemate had been broken for the first time since 1914, setting in motion the end of the war in 1918.

ORS

Despite its diminutive size, Ors played an important role in the war.

GETTING THERE AND AWAY From Calais **by car**, follow the A26/E15 southeast to Cambrai, then take D643 to Ors (*182km; approx 2hrs 5mins*). Ors does have a station, but **trains** are very infrequent.

WHAT TO SEE AND DO
Wilfred Owen Memorial (*La Maison Forestière, Route Départementale 959;* ☏ *03 27 84 54 83;* ⊕ *10.00–13.00 & 14.00–17.00 Mon & Wed–Sat, 14.00–17.00 1st Sun of each month, closed 15 Nov–15 Apr; ask mayor for appointment; free entry*) Jacky Duminy, the Mayor of Ors, commissioned Turner Prize-nominee Simon Patterson to create this memorial to the great poet in 1991. It's a startling, almost surreal, white snail shell-shaped structure with a ramp leading to an airy space lit from above. Onto its walls, etched in a skin of glass, is Wilfred Owen's *Dulce et Decorum Est* – his best-known poem that was published posthumously in 1920. As the lights dim, the voice of actor Kenneth Branagh recites 12 of Owen's poems, with silences in between. The performance lasts an hour.

Wilfred Owen Memorial (LNT)

Leaving the room, you walk down into the original dark, dank cellar in the hut where Owen and 29 others slept on his last night alive. It was here he wrote reassuring his mother that 'there is no danger down here.'

A 6km Wilfred Owen Remembrance Trail also starts from the museum and a free English-language audio guide can be downloaded onto smartphones from www.tourisme-cambresis.fr. A note about practicalities: the museum is pretty remote, so if you're in need of refreshment drop in at the **Estaminet de l'Ermitage** (*Route Départementale 959, Le Bois l'Evèque;* \ *03 27 77 99 48;* ⏲ *10.00–15.00 Tue–Thu, 10.00–21.00 Fri–Sat)* for a reliable and inexpensive lunch of local specialties.

LE QUESNOY

Part of the green Avesnois region, Le Quesnoy (pronounced 'kenwaw') provided a break from the horrors of the trenches and the Germans happily held onto Le Nord region's best-protected walled town until a week before the Armistice, when it was reclaimed by a band of brave Kiwis.

TOURIST INFORMATION

Le Quesnoy Tourist Office 1 Rue du Maréchal Joffre; \ 03 27 20 54 70; www.tourisme-lequesnoy.com; ⏲ 09.00–12.00 & 14.00–18.00 Mon–Fri, 10.00–12.30 & 15.00–18.00 Sat–Sun & public holidays

GETTING THERE AND AWAY From Calais **by car** , follow the E40/A16 towards Dunkerque, branch onto A25/E42 towards Lille/Rijsel. South of Lille, take A23 to Valenciennes, then follow A2, then D649, then branch onto D934 south to Le Quesnoy (*175km; approx 1hr 50mins)*. Regular weekday **rail** services depart from Lille Flandres (*1hr)*.

WHAT TO SEE AND DO

New Zealand Memorial (*Rue Jeanne d'Arc, or L'Avenue des Néo-Zélandais*) A week before the November 1918 Armistice, a group of New Zealand soldiers liberated Le Quesnoy in an act worthy of James Bond himself. It would be New Zealand's last major action of the war.

At 05.30 on 4 November, under heavy mortar fire and smoke from burning oil drums, a few soldiers from the Fourth Battalion Third Rifle Brigade attempted to scale the town's ramparts by propping up a ladder, but this proved too short, so they used a narrow stone wall to cross the surrounding moat instead.

At the same time Captain Napier, a mortar expert, shelled the top of the walls. By 16.00, bewildered German soldiers faced an onslaught by rampart-scaling Kiwis. After strong resistance, during which the New Zealand Division suffered 400 casualties, with 93 killed in action, the 1,500 Germans surrendered. Sixty-five of the New Zealanders who died here are buried in Le Quesnoy. Pinned to the ramparts is a carved relief panel depicting the dramatic events, an angel watching over the soldiers and a silver fern – the Kiwi national emblem.

None of the 55,000 French residents at the time lost their lives and their gratitude remains as strong as ever: *Teko Teko* – the town's Maori giant, given to the town in 1972 by the New Zealand Rifle Brigade – shares pride of place with Pierre Bimberlot, Le Quesnoy's wicker giant.

MAUBEUGE/FEIGNIES

Despite being heavily fortified, this major iron and steel district, situated on the Sambre River, was heavily hammered in both World War I and II – it still shows.

TOURIST INFORMATION

Maubeuge Tourist Office Porte de Mons, Pl Vauban; ☏ 03 27 62 11 93; http://uk.maubeuge-tourisme.com; ⏱ Jul–Sep 09.00–12.30 & 13.30–18.00 Mon–Fri, 09.00–12.30 & 13.30–17.00 Sat, 09.30–1.30 Sun; Oct–Jun 09.00–12.30 & 13.30–17.00 Mon–Sat

GETTING THERE AND AWAY From Calais **by car**, follow the E40/A16 towards Dunkerque, branch onto A25/E42 towards Lille/Rijsel. South of Lille, take A23 to Valenciennes, then follow D649 east past Bavay to Maubeuge (*194km; approx 2hrs*). Regular **rail** services depart from Valenciennes (*40mins*) and from Lille (*1hr 20mins*).

WHAT TO SEE AND DO

Fort de Leveau (*Rue de Mairieux, Feignies;* ☏ 03 27 62 37 07; http://fortdeleveau. voila.net; ⏱ *Apr–Oct 13.00– 17.00 Mon–Fri, 14.30–18.00 last two Sundays of the month; guided tours start at 15.00; closed holidays except 11 Nov 14.30–18.00; adult/ child/under 10s €5/1.50/free*) One of 11 fortified positions surrounding the town of **Maubeuge** – just 9km from the Belgian border – Leveau Fort in Feignies stood at a key intersection of the Brussels–Liège railway line to Paris. Early in World War I the German Army, who were eager to press on to the French capital for a quick victory over France, had it in their sights. They were hindered by the Allied forces of France, Belgium and Britain, but after a two-week siege between 27 August and 7 September 1914 – the longest of its kind in World War I – Leveau Fort's defenders were forced to surrender when the 60,000-strong German troops flattened the outer fortifications with shells fired from long-range German guns. Nevertheless, Allied Forces had prevented a hefty number of German soldiers from taking part in the First Battle of the Marne (see box, page 86), which began on 5 September.

A fixed bridge and drawbridge, destroyed by the shelling, will be rebuilt to commemorate the siege and will be inaugurated on 6 September 2014.

Fort de Leveau (LNT)

Pas-de-Calais: Arras, Lens and the Ports

ARRAS

Arras was central to some of the fiercest fighting of World War I and reduced to ruin in the conflict. Not that you would notice now, such was the brilliance in rebuilding from the rubble replicas of the glorious 17th- and 18th-century gabled buildings around the cobbled twin squares. Today, the capital of Pas-de-Calais is positively cosmopolitan and an ideal centre for exploring the battlefields.

GETTING THERE AND AWAY Travelling **by car** from the Calais ferry, follow the A26/E15 south (*112km; approx 1hr*). For **trains** from Gare Lille Europe, change platforms for the fast TGV service to Arras (*30mins*); there are also regular trains from Gare Lille Flandres (*1hr*).

TOURIST INFORMATION

Arras tourist office trains and works with a number of local guides and can arrange **battlefield tours** on your behalf. Alternatively, you could contact the Guild of Battlefield Guides for more information (*www.gbg-international.com*).

Arras Tourist Office Town Hall, Pl des Héros; \ 03 21 51 26 95; www.explorearras.com; ⊕ mid Sep–31 Mar 10.00–12.00 & 14.00–18.00 Mon, 09.00–12.00 & 14.00–18.00 Tue–Sat, 10.00–12.30 & 14.30–18.30 Sun; 1 Apr–mid Sep 09.00–18.30 Mon–Sat, 10.00–13.00 & 14.30–18.30 Sun. Free maps & accommodation information. See website for city passes & guided tours featuring World War I sites.

WHAT TO SEE AND DO
Wellington Quarry (Carrière Wellington) (*Rue Arthur Delétoile;* \ *03 21 51 26 95; www.explorearras.com;* ⊕ *10.00–12.30 & 13.30–18.00 daily, closed for a month following Christmas; adult/child €6.80/3.10; audio-guide tours available & also regular guided tours*) These carefully preserved British Army tunnels were used throughout the war and connect with tunnels and quarries dating back in some cases to the Roman era.

It was through here and similar tunnels that some 24,000 soldiers emerged, blinking in the early morning sleet of Easter Monday, 9 April 1917, to fight an unsuspecting enemy in the Battle of Arras (see box, opposite).

Housed in one of the original medieval subterranean chalk quarries, the two interconnecting labyrinths were created by 500 New Zealanders, predominantly Maori coal and gold miners, aided by 'bantams' – Yorkshire miners who didn't meet the Army's minimum-height requirement of five feet three inches. But amid the post-war chaos and the wish to forget, they lay forgotten until 1990 when Alain

In 1917 Arras was under Allied control, but the town had been taking a pasting since October 1914. A tantalising salient – the military term for a pocket of ground that juts into enemy territory – had developed and Field Marshal Douglas Haig (see box, page 63) and his French counterpart needed to devise a way to breach the German line. Arras, they decided, would be used in a diversionary offensive, drawing in enemy reserves for several days before the French launched a large-scale bid to break the enemy stranglehold on the Chemin des Dames ridge in the Champagne region (see page 77).

There was one big snag: how could the Allies concentrate a large number of troops near the Front Line without arousing suspicion? Fearful of the slaughter experienced in the battles of Verdun and the Somme, the commanders suggested a daring solution: to create a vast network of tunnels enabling troops to emerge directly in front of the German line rather than facing the deadly machine-gun fire of No Man's Land.

So at 05.30 on 9 April 1917, an enormous explosion was the signal for more than 24,000 men to surge from their underground hiding places to appear directly in front of enemy lines. There was no time for the Germans to raise the alarm. Some were still found in their pyjamas in a nearby village.

Though the first few days were a tactical success, with the Germans forced to fall back on their second line of defence, it proved a costly offensive. Heavy reinforcements led to vigorous counterattacks and a series of bloody battles, but the Allies were able to push the combat zone back some ten kilometres and relieve the pressure on Arras. More than 150,000 British casualties were reported between April and May 1917; total losses for the Germans are presumed to have been around the same. While the ground advancements were impressive considering the Western Front stalemate, the high losses and ultimate failure of the Allied offensive overshadowed the gains.

The battle will perhaps be best remembered for the taking of **Vimy Ridge**, when four Canadian divisions of the British Army separately set out on the same day to conquer the 145m-high ridge – dubbed 'The Pimple'– whose position allowed the Germans to fire freely at Allied forces. Heavily fortified, with several lines of trenches punctuated with concrete shelters, the ridge had proved impenetrable – all previous attempts to take the hilltop fortress had failed.

However, in the months leading up to the attack, the Canadians had dug a ten-kilometre network of tunnels that ran to the Front. Within 30 minutes of the attack, their path cleared by cannon fire and tanks, the Canadian divisions had overrun part of the German Front Line and, within an hour, parts of the second too.

By the middle of the afternoon, despite heavy losses inflicted during the initial wave, they controlled most of the ridge. The next day they took possession of Hill 145, where the famous memorial now stands (see page 55). Two days later, the whole ridge was under Allied control and the Germans had been forced back into the surrounding coal basin. The Canadians took 3,400 prisoners in three days along a 14km stretch. It was an outright victory, but losses were high: between 9 and 14 April, 10,600 men were either killed or wounded.

Wellington Quarry (DG)

Jacques, in charge of Arras's archaeology department, decided to investigate the *boves* (caves) in which a few locals sheltered during World War II.

'It was so exciting to find history undisturbed,' he said. 'The first time we opened the tunnel we found an operating theatre, boots, helmets, dog-tags and even bullets that had been removed from wounded soldiers.'

Along with Jean-Marie Prestaux, the enthusiastic former director of tourism, Jacques worked out that one quarry, known as Wellington – one of a number named after the Kiwi tunnellers and home to the Suffolk Regiment – lay under a former council-owned campsite, allowing for reconstruction to take place. The others had either collapsed, were unsafe, or in some cases, had houses built over them.

The €4-million **museum** now offers a 75-minute tour evoking the underground privations leading up to the fateful spring offensive. After a short introduction, accompanied by a bilingual expert and equipped with audio-guides, visitors take a glass-walled lift 20m down to the tunnels into a compelling Great War world where drawings, faded photos and graffiti bring a terrifying touch of authenticity. Everywhere cans and old stone jars lie discarded and two large rusting buckets rest discreetly beneath wooden holes, above which the word 'latrine' is written.

Particularly poignant are the copies of letters home. Writing to his wife and baby son, Private Harry Holland scribbled: 'Kiss our Harry for me. When I see him again, it will take me all my time to catch him.' But Private Holland never returned.

AROUND ARRAS

SAINT-LAURENT-BLANGY
German Military Cemetery (*Chemin de Bailleul;* ⊕ *daily; free entry*) Black crosses mark the graves of 7,069 German soldiers who died during the Great War, while a mass grave contains the remains of 24,870 soldiers, over half of whom were never identified. When the remains of a further 4,283 soldiers were moved from the German section of Comines Cemetery near Lille, it became the second-largest German cemetery in France (after La Maison Blanche, see page 57) – home to over 36,000 souls.

MONCHY-LE-PREUX
Newfoundland Memorial (*Rue de Chaussy;* ⊕ *daily; free entry*) Standing atop a German post in the centre of town, this bronze statue of a caribou is one of five (there's another in Beaumont-Hamel, page 70), erected in honour of the Newfoundland soldiers who took part in World War I – at the time, Newfoundland was still part of the British Empire.

MONT-SAINT-ÉLOI

Ruined towers and lookout (*Rue de la Mairie; ☉ daily; free entry*) An abbey was established here in the 7th century but pillaged for its stone during the Revolution. When World War I broke out, all that remained of the abbey were the twin towers of the west wall. Nevertheless, these towers provided an invaluable lookout point for the French, who could see the German lines set up on Vimy Ridge and Lorette Spur. Heavy shelling during the war shortened the towers by about 10m and the ruins today are a living monument to the destruction and devastation caused by war.

VIMY

Canadian National Vimy Memorial (*Route départementale 55; follow signs from Vimy, off the N17 reached via junction 7 on the E15/A26; ☉ year round; free entry*) It's difficult not to be deeply affected by the Vimy Memorial. The white twin-columned monument, seemingly soaring to the sky, stands alone in open country slightly north of the 240-acre Canadian Memorial Park (see below), of which it forms a part. The stone structure commemorates not just the Battle of Vimy Ridge but also the 66,000 Canadians killed overall in the Great War, of which 11,285 have no known graves. It took 11 years and US$1.5 million to build, and the memorial rests on a bed of 11,000 tonnes of concrete reinforced with hundreds of tonnes of steel. The work of Toronto sculptor and designer Walter Seymour Allward, it was unveiled on 26 July 1936 by King Edward VIII.

The towering columns each stand 45m high: one bears a maple leaf, the other a *fleur-de-lys* – these symbolise the sacrifice of both Canada and France, respectively. The columns and the sculptured figures (created by Canadian artists) together contain almost 6,000 tonnes of limestone brought from an abandoned Roman quarry on the Adriatic Sea, in present-day Croatia. The largest piece, carved from a 30-tonne block, shows a grieving figure of a woman representing Canada in mourning. The memorial ultimately provided Canada's previously divided provinces with a true sense of national identity in relation to their shared war history.

Canadian Memorial Park This area of parkland on the territory of the commune of Givenchy-en-Gohelle was granted to Canada by the French in 1922. Here among 11,285 Canadian trees and shrubs – reflecting the number of Canadians missing in war – families stroll over grass-covered shell holes and mine craters. Others play games or jog along gravel paths that run alongside one huge crater, which at first glance could be mistaken for a golf-course bunker. The crater is one of 14 created when the hidden Allied mines exploded on Easter Monday, 9 April 1917, during the Battle of Arras (see box, page 53).

Sand-bagged trenches in which visitors can now walk indicate the closeness of the German and Allied front lines, which in places were just 25m apart.

A huge number of artillery shells were fired into the area around Vimy Ridge. Many did not explode and remain dangerous to this day, with red zone areas remaining fenced off to visitors, though the sheep graze happily enough in them.

The **visitor centre** (☏ *03 21 50 68 68; ☉ late Jan–Feb 09.00–17.00 daily; Mar–24 Oct 10.00–18.00 daily; 25 Oct–13 Dec 09.00–17.00 daily; closed public holidays;*

Canadian National Vimy Memorial (PCT)

free entry), manned by Canadian students, features comprehensive displays in English. Free guided tours are available Tuesday to Sunday during opening hours.

ABLAIN-SAINT-NAZAIRE
Notre-Dame de Lorette French National War Cemetery (*Ablain-Saint-Nazaire, signposted off the D937 between Arras & Béthune;* ⏰ *08.00–18.30; free entry*)
France's largest military cemetery contains over 20,000 gravestones in addition to eight communal graves in which a further 22,000 unknown soldiers are buried.

Situated on a plateau, it has a remarkable view of the eastern part of the Gohelle Plain dominated by twin slag heaps, known as 11/19, and the Artois hills in the west. On the summit sits a new **Memorial to The Great War** – one of the world's largest – inscribed with the names of 600,000 men who died on all sides. The ring design is the work of Parisian architect Philippe Prost and is carved with a human chain in which former allies and foes of all nationalities, listed in alphabetical order, link hands.

Musée Vivant 14/18 (*Colline de Notre-Dame-de-Lorette, behind the cemetery;* ✎ *03 21 45 15 80;* ⏰ *09.00–18.00 daily; admission €6.10/3.30 adult/child*) This museum traces the daily experiences of Great War soldiers, containing a collection of more than 300 items, reconstructed underground shelters and a recreated battlefield covering more than 1,000m of trenches. Organised bilingual activities are arranged in English and French.

SOUCHEZ
Exhibition centre and tourist information office (*At the foot of the Notre-Dame-de-Lorette hill*) Due to open in late 2014, this centre will have World War I exhibits and memorabilia as well as terminals that will provide visitors with background information on the soldiers whose names are listed. Further information will be available on our updates website closer to the opening date; see box, page 9, for details.

Cabaret-Rouge British Cemetery (*1.5km south of Souchez on the west side of the D937 Arras–Béthune road*) Named after the red-brick Cabaret Rouge café located nearby, the cemetery served as one of a small number of 'open cemeteries' where the remains of fallen servicemen, newly discovered in the region, were buried. Today, the cemetery contains over 7,650 burials from World War I – over half of which remain unidentified. They include those of British, Irish, Australian, New Zealand, Indian and South African soldiers; it is also the final resting place for over 70 officers of the Royal Flying Corps and Royal Air Force.

Cabaret-Rouge also has a particularly close connection to the Canadian Infantry, with hundreds of those killed at Vimy Ridge buried here. In May 2000, the remains of an unknown Canadian soldier were taken from this cemetery and buried in a special tomb at the foot of the National War Memorial in Ottawa, Canada.

In anticipation of the World War I centenary, major renovation works started in May 2013, with headstones replaced and borders replanted.

Notre-Dame de Lorette (PCT)

La Maison Blanche German War Cemetery, Neuville-Saint-Vaast (DG)

NEUVILLE-SAINT-VAAST
La Maison Blanche German War Cemetery (*Route de Béthune, Neuville-Saint-Vaast; 8km off D973/D55 to Béthune*) This is the largest German war cemetery in France, with a total of 44,843 soldiers buried beneath black crosses each bearing the names of four individuals. Only 8,040 remain unidentified and these unknown souls are buried in a mass grave. A relief map at the entrance represents the battlefield on which the cemetery was built.

AROUND LENS

LOOS-EN-GOHELLE
Musée 14/18 Alexandre Villedieu (*14/18 Pl de la République, Loos-en-Gohelle;* ℡ *03 21 70 59 75/03 21 28 99 82;* e *a.villedieu@wanadoo.fr;* ⊕ *09.00–11.00 &14.00–17.00 daily; reservations required for admission, entry €3; guided tours €6/group of 5 minimum, €5/groups of 10 or more*) A fascinating display of souvenirs and everyday objects from the battlefield populate this museum, grouped by nationality. The soldiers' possessions were collected by an association, 'Loos sur les traces de la Grande Guerre', and the president of the association, Alfred Duparcq, provides lively anecdotes (in French), including the story of how a piece of wood used by a soldier to defend himself came from the altar of Loos church.

Dud Corner Cemetery (*Route de Béthune, 1km west of Loos;* ⊕ *all year; free entry*) This cemetery contains the graves of over 2,000 soldiers, of which over half are unidentified – most were killed in the Battle of Loos. At the back stands the semi-circular **Loos Memorial** engraved with the names of 20,000 soldiers with no known graves who fell in the Lys River area. The name 'Dud Corner' possibly stems from the number of unexploded enemy shells found following the Armistice.

HAISNES
St Mary's Advanced Dressing Station Cemetery (*Follow the Commonwealth War Graves Commission sign on the D947 Lens to La Bassée Rd; the cemetery lies off this on the D39 Hulloch to Vermelles Rd;* ℡ *03 21 25 43 43;* ⊕ *year round; free entry*) The village of Haisnes-lez-La Bassé was nearly reached by the 9th (Scottish) and 7th Divisions on the first day of the Battle of Loos. The battlefield clearance cemetery, which lies in farmland, was created after the Armistice; the great majority of the graves are of those killed in action between September and October 1915.

HARNES
Musée d'Histoire et d'Archéologie (*50 Rue André Deprez;* ℡ *03 21 49 02 29;* ⊕ *14.00–17.00 Mon–Sat; entrance fee*) This small museum is housed in a late 19th-century mansion and has four rooms devoted to both World Wars, as well as a photographic exhibition showing how the town changed between 1900 and 1950. To get there, buses No. 14, 16 and 120 depart Lens regularly (8km).

The brutal Battle of Loos (appropriately pronounced 'Loss') was fought between 25 September and 4 November 1915. Like those at Arras and Vimy Ridge, the battle was part of the wider **Artois–Loos Offensive** which, conducted by the British and French, was sometimes known as the Third Battle of Artois. It was launched simultaneously with the main French offensive in Champagne.

Six divisions were committed to the attack, despite Douglas Haig's (see box, page 63) fears over a worrying shortage of shells and exhaustion among his troops. He was even more concerned about the difficult terrain that needed crossing, but his troops far outnumbered the Germans and thus the odds seemed in the Allies's favour. However, having failed to 'soften' enemy trenches with a four-day barrage of 250,000 shells, the British used gas for the first time. The Germans had used it previously in the Battle of Ypres with success, but, in a cruel twist of fate, a change in wind direction blew 140 tonnes of British-deployed chlorine gas back onto British lines. Many soldiers, unable to see through their fogged-up inefficient masks, removed them, which led to seven deaths; another 2,600 had to be withdrawn from the front line as a result. The attempted gas attack was an unmitigated disaster.

Meanwhile, the southern end of the attack proved to be a spectacular success. British troops, predominantly Scots, took the village of Loos and Hill 70 under the cover of smokescreens and advanced towards Lens. However, a delay due to lack of munitions and the late arrival of reinforcements allowed the Germans to retake Hill 70. Further to the north the British advance was slowed by the formidable defences of the **Hohenzollern Redoubt** – a vast complex of trenches, underground shelters and machine-gun nests. Even so, the British managed to take part of the German line at the front, but the next day German reinforcements arrived in huge numbers to fill the breaches.

By 28 September, after sporadic fighting for several days, the British general staff gave the order to abandon positions taken the previous day. Another offensive on 13 October again opened with a gas attack but came to a similarly disastrous end in poor weather conditions. In a mere ten minutes, the 46th Division lost 180 officers and 3,583 men in an attempt to take the Hohenzollern Redoubt. Overall, British casualties at Loos totalled 50,000, including at least 20,000 dead; the Germans lost some 25,000 men. The nature of the fighting also meant that most of the dead were unrecoverable from the battlefield until after the war, three years later. By then, their bodies were unidentifiable, and many cemeteries around Loos contain a high percentage of unknown graves.

The failure at Loos also led to the British Commander in Chief Sir John French being replaced by General Haig (see box, page 63) in December 1915. The battlefield is situated 5km northwest of the former mining town of Lens, near the village of Loos-en-Gohelle, off A26 at junction 6 or junction 6.1; follow the signs via the D943.

ESCALLES

Moving to France's northern coast, the tranquil landscape that accompanies a drive along the D940 belies the area's centrally important position during the war: the cross-Channel ports were instrumental in keeping Allied supplies flowing as the Germans attempted to close the shipping routes.

GETTING THERE AND AWAY Bus No.5 departs from outside Calais theatre and stops in Cap Blanc-Nez in summer, just up the hill from Escalles, and in Sangatte the rest of the year.

WHAT TO SEE AND DO
The Dover Patrol Monument (*Cap Blanc-Nez, D940 north of Escalles, towards Sangatte*) This monument pays tribute to the assortment of Tribal-class destroyer boats, armed trawlers, drifters, yachts and motorboats that joined up with submarines and seaplanes to defend the Strait of Dover from the German Navy throughout World War I. The Patrol kept the waterways navigable and escorted hospital and troop ships, as well laying and keeping the sea free of mines. Throughout 1917 the Dover Patrol prevented U boats from leaving German-held ports in Belgium and between 22 and 23 April 1918, it raided Zeebrugge and Ostend. A certain Captain ER Evans is remembered for carrying a penguin mascot nailed to the mast of his destroyer – a relic from his days with Captain Scott's ill-fated Antarctic Expedition.

BOULOGNE-SUR-MER

Boulogne-sur-Mer was one of the top three cross-Channel ports that received supplies and troops in World War I. It became an enormous barracks, with public buildings requisitioned to house the wounded evacuated from the Front.

GETTING THERE AND AWAY From Calais **by car**, follow the E402/A16 southwest past Marquise (*34km; approx 30mins*). There are two SNCF **railway stations**:

MY SON JACK

The short life of John (Jack) Kipling, the son of esteemed British poet Rudyard Kipling, was brought to life by *Harry Potter* star Daniel Radcliffe in the much-acclaimed British TV drama *My Boy Jack*.

Aged just 18, Jack died on 27 September 1915 during the Battle of Loos, but whether the grave bearing his name in St Mary's Advanced Dressing Station Cemetery – a post-war battlefield *(W)* clearance cemetery (see page 57) – is correct has been a matter of much debate. This is mostly due to the rank displayed on the deceased officer's uniform, which was that of a second lieutenant: Jack had been promoted to a full lieutenant. Scholars speculate as to whether his promotion to the higher rank was never gazetted on his arrival in France, hence the error on the gravestone.

There's also confusion regarding the location of the body. Jack Kipling was last seen about a mile and three-quarters southeast of where the cemetery now lies, yet the body listed as his was found about two miles to the southwest. There's even some question as to whether the uniform of the deceased officer, originally described simply as 'a lieutenant of the Irish Guards' was actually that of the Irish Guards.

It was not until June 1992 that the Commonwealth War Graves Commission finally decided that the 'lieutenant' buried had to be Kipling because they could account for all the others who had died during the battle.

Jack's story illustrates the dangers of unbridled patriotism, but reflects the ultimate sacrifice made by so many young soldiers.

8

15–20-minute walk from Boulogne station to the town centre. Some slow trains stop at Boulogne Tintelleries station.

WHAT TO SEE AND DO

Boulogne Eastern Cemetery (*Rue de Dringhen;* ⊕ *Oct–15 Mar 08.00–18.00 daily, 16 Mar–Sep 08.00–19.00 daily; free entry*) The cemetery contains 5,821 Commonwealth graves (some contain more than one body) of which 5,577 date from World War I and 224 from World War II.

One grave is that of poet **Julian Grenfell** who, in 1914, shocked many by likening the war to 'a big picnic without the objectlessness of a picnic', claiming he had 'never been so well or so happy'. His most famous poem, 'Into Battle', was published on 26 May 1915, a few days after his death in a Boulogne hospital from a shrapnel wound to the head. He was 27 years old.

In spring 1918, with the cemetery at maximum capacity, a new one was opened in the village of Terlincthun near Wimille (north of Boulogne-sur-Mer). After the war, Terlincthun took in graves from isolated plots which could not be adequately maintained. This explains how 200 soldiers from Russia, Poland and the USA, as well as German prisoners of war, lie alongside 4,378 British, Indian and Canadian Commonwealth graves (of which 3,380 are identified).

A further 48 graves belong to members of the Royal Air Force who were killed in September 1918 above the town of **Marquise** – northeast of Boulogne-sur-Mer – during a German bombing raid. It is a stark reminder that the Great War opened up a new battleground – the sky – in which the Royal Flying Corps played a major role.

Around Boulogne-sur-Mer

Wimereux Communal Cemetery (*Rue Jean Moulin*) Situated 6km north of Boulogne, this cemetery is the site of 2,847 graves of soldiers and nurses who died in the ten British Army field hospitals in the area.

Among them stands the headstone of Lieutenant-Colonel John McCrae, a Canadian doctor and poet who cared for soldiers wounded in the Second Battle of Ypres and who wrote the famous poem 'In Flanders Fields' (see box, page 19).

Saint-Etienne-au-Mont Communal Cemetery (*Rue Edmond Madaré, Saint-Etienne-au-Mont;* ⊕ *daily; free entry*) The rows of white headstones may look like those of a standard Commonwealth cemetery, but in fact they're erected in honour of 160 members of the Chinese Labour Corps (and ten members of the South African Labour Corps). The Labour Corps were made up of civilians who carried out manual tasks, such as felling timber, unloading boat cargo, maintaining railways, etc, freeing up British soldiers for fighting. It must have been incredibly isolating for the Chinese labourers,

The Dover Patrol Monument, Escalles (PCT)

Boulogne-sur-Mer Tourist Office Parvis de Nausicaà; Boulevard Sainte Beuve; ☏ 03 21 10 88 10; www.tourisme-boulognesurmer.com; ⏰ mid Nov–Mar 10.30–12.30 & 14.00–17.30 Mon–Sat; Apr–mid Nov 10.00–12.30 & 13.45–18.00 Mon–Sat, 10.30–13.00 & 14.30–17.00 Sun; Jul–Aug 10.00–19.00 Mon–Sat, 10.30–13.00 & 14.30–18.00 Sun

who didn't speak English, yet by the end of the war there were over 96,000 in British Army service. To get to the cemetery from Boulogne-sur-Mer, take Marineo bus No E or No 1.

ÉTAPLES-SUR-MER

Seen as relatively safe from attack, the protected port of Étaples was selected as the site of a vast training camp thanks to its good rail links to both the northern and southern battlefields. But according to many stationed the along Western Front, Étaples – or 'Eat Apples' as it was nicknamed – was reckoned to be the most detested of all base camps.

In 1917, 100,000 troops were camped here with a variety of hospitals equipped to deal with 22,000 wounded or sick. Conditions at the camp were atrocious, and both recruits and battle-weary veterans were subjected to intensive training at the notorious Bull Ring training camp set among the sand dunes. After two weeks, many of the wounded were only too glad to return to the Front with unhealed wounds. There were even clashes between patients and the Military Police.

GETTING THERE AND AWAY Take the **train** to Le Touquet Paris-Plage and walk the 1km to Étaples. Catch **bus** No 42 from Boulogne-sur-Mer (in the direction of Berck) to Étaples; buses depart from Place de France Monday to Saturday at 08.05, 10.35, 13.40, 16.00 and 18.25 (*1hr*).

WHAT TO SEE AND DO
Étaples Military Cemetery (*2km northwest of Étaples off the D940;* ⏰ *year round; free entry*) Terraced rows of white gravestones provide a grim reminder that, of 11,500 interred here, 10,771 died in or around Étaples during World War I, the earliest dating from May 1915. The tombs recall soldiers from Canada, Australia, New Zealand, South Africa and India as well as 658 German burials. Thirty-five burials remain unidentified.

A further 119 individuals were buried here after World War II – of which 38 remain unidentified – which makes this the largest Commonwealth cemetery in France. Sir Edwin Lutyens designed the towering white-stone arches at the entrance. There is a visitor's book where you can leave a message: 'So sad I never met you, Dad' and 'At last I meet you, Granddad' are typical of many. A register

Étaples Military Cemetery (PCT)

shows the location of each grave. Essential renovations to the terraces were underway at the time of writing.

MONTREUIL-SUR-MER

Once a port connected to the sea before the River Canche silted up, Montreuil-sur-Mer became the nerve centre of the British Army in March 1916, after it had been initially set up in St-Omer in October 1914. Divided into five departments, this vast general headquarters was staffed by a wide range of military personnel and forced this previously sleepy old fortified town into playing a pivotal role in the war.

GETTING THERE AND AWAY By **car**, either join the E402/A16 at Calais and leave at exit 29 for the D901 and the 75km journey, which is toll free, or continue on the E402/A16 and leave at exit 26 for the D939/D901, which might be slightly quicker but is subject to a €2.70 toll each way on the Boulogne stretch of the motorway. If arriving at Calais by **train**, take the frequent TER service from Calais-Ville station to Boulogne-Ville and change to the TER Line 14 (Arras via Étaples and St-Pol) for Montreuil-sur-Mer station, which is just a few hundred metres down from the ramparts. There are nine trains daily from 04.00 to around 18.30 and the journey takes between 30 and 50 minutes.

If travelling from Lille Flandres, take the TER Line 15 (Boulogne via St-Pol and Béthune). Trains are less frequent but the journey time is around the same.

WHAT TO SEE AND DO
La Citadelle (General Headquarters) (*Rue Carnot;* 03 21 86 90 83; ⊕ *Mar, Oct & Nov 10.00–12.00 & 14.00–17.00, Apr–Sep 10.00–12.00 & 14.00–18.00, Dec–Feb closed; adult/child €4.50/3, free audio-guide & touchpad tours*) In 1916, this fortified citadel became Field Marshal Douglas Haig's (see box, opposite) operational headquarters, supplying troops with provisions and equipment from Dunkerque, Calais and Boulogne for the Front in Flanders, Artois and the Somme. An exhibition, held in the casemates of the citadel and entitled 'A Friendly Invasion', illuminates the immense scale of operations and communications which supported the British Expeditionary Force with munitions, transport, food, communications and medical services. It will run from 1 March to 6 October 2014.

General Headquarters Museum (*Hôtel Loysel Le Gaucher, Rue Victor Dubourg*)
This brand-new heritage centre is scheduled to open in 2016. It will reveal the huge

A former cavalry commander, Haig was born to a middle-class family in Edinburgh in 1861 and rose to become commander of the British Expeditionary Force (British Army) in 1915 until the end of the war. During the war his leadership wasn't faulted, but some historians now question his inability to alter tactics and embrace new technologies, which possibly led to the unnecessary deaths of millions of soldiers – many of the battles he led counted among the bloodiest of the entire war.

'behind-the-scenes' operations that gave vital support to the troops in the field and show how the final outcome of the war depended as much on the work of men and women behind the lines as it did on the courage and weaponry of the troops. Check the updates website (see box, page 9) for further information when available.

Haig statue (*Place du Théâtre*) In the centre of this square stands an equestrian statue of Field Marshal Douglas Haig (see box, above), who commandeered Beaurepaire House a few kilometres away and had a penchant for riding through the adjoining countryside. The statue was taken down during the German occupation in World War II, but locals recovered the original mould and recast a new one.

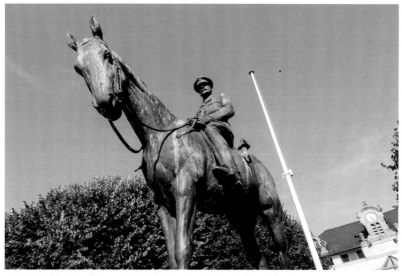

Field Marshal Douglas Haig statue, Montreuil-sur-Mer (PCT)

Pas-de-Calais: Arras, Lens and the Ports   MONTREUIL-SUR-MER

8

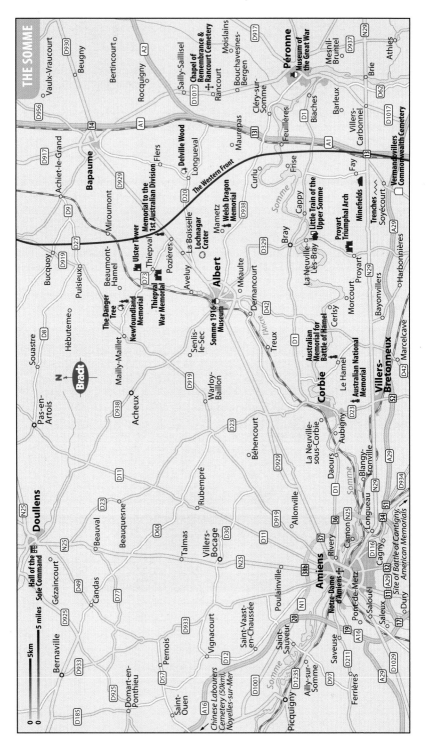

THE SOMME

9

The Somme

Of all the areas in France, the Somme is perhaps the most tragically associated with the Great War. Soldiers described its battlefields as a land of 'foul brown mush, which swallows everything'. The most notable of the battles here was the Somme Offensive, which began in July 1916 and, in five months, claimed well over 1,000,000 casualties, approximately 420,000 British, nearly 200,000 French and 650,000 German (see box, page 66). The region has 410 Commonwealth, 22 French and 14 German cemeteries.

BATTLEFIELD TOURS

Battlefields Experience \ 03 22 76 29 60; www.battlefieldsexperience.co.uk. Run by boy solider & military historian Rod Bedford.
Chemins d'Histoire Battlefield Tours \ 03 23 67 77 64; www.cheminsdhistoire.com. Bespoke or private tours that can be themed according to your nationality.
Cobbers Battlefield Tours \ 06 87 43 10 49; www.anzac-tours.com. Small-group minibus tours departing from the Somme 1916 Museum in Albert, including buggy & cycling tours. Led by Brit Colin Gillard.
Ibis Albert \ 03 22 75 52 52. This Ibis hotel in Albert runs 2–3hr battlefield tours for groups.

Rajouter Cycling the Western Front \ 07 88 24 59 01; www.cyclingthewesternfront.co.uk
Skylark Battlefield Tours \ 03 22 85 14 56; www.lesaloutettes.net. Run by personable UK owners Vic & Diane.
Somme(r)–Ballade \ 03 22 75 25 01; www.somme-r-ballade.jimdo.com. Somme walking tours led by Julia Maasen conducted in French, English & German.
Terres de Mémoire \ 03 22 84 23 05; www.terresdememoire.com. Another 2-man team offering in-depth tours of the Somme.
True Blue Digger Tours \ 03 22 51 56 21; www.trueblue-diggertours.com. Half- & full-day tours catering to Australians.

THE CHRISTMAS TRUCE OF 1914

Stories of a Christmas Truce in 1914 are partly true. Along a few sections of the Western Front, unofficial ceasefires took place between British and German forces. On Christmas Eve, some British infantrymen were astonished to see Christmas trees decorated with candles glowing behind enemy lines and to hear the sound of carols drifting across the mud. In a few stretches of No Man's Land an exchange of greetings and even small gifts began and for a brief spell there was peace. Sir Arthur Conan Doyle, in his history of 1914, saluted the Christmas Truce as 'one human episode amid all the atrocities which have stained the memory of the war'. Did the enemy forces actually play football against each other? In one or two places, yes. A member of the 1/6th Cheshire Regiment referred to a game in his war diary, and a 3–2 victory to the Germans!

AMIENS

Surprisingly, the Great War left the grand historic capital of Picardy relatively unscathed, despite it being a hive of war-related activity, from Germans seizing hostages here during the first months of the war to the Thanksgiving Mass held in its cathedral on 18 November 1918. There was even a guidebook about the great city on the Somme printed in English for soldiers.

GETTING THERE AND AWAY Coming **by car** from Calais, follow the E402/A16 south, past Boulogne-sur-Mer and Abbeville, to Amiens (*158km; approx 1hr30mins*). From Calais, Lille or Paris-Gare du Nord, **trains** take approximately one hour to reach Amiens.

BATTLE OF THE SOMME (SOMME OFFENSIVE)

Up until 1916, the Somme just witnessed skirmishes. However, late in 1915, the Allies planned a set of major offensives against the Central Powers; the Franco-British were to focus on breaking through the Front Line in the Somme. At the same time, though, the German Army decided to switch its main attention from the Eastern to the Western Front, aiming to draw the French Army into a devastating battle around Verdun in early 1916 (see box, page 88). As a result, many French troops were sent east to the Meuse in the first half of the year, while the British Army became the principal Allied force involved in the Somme Offensive, which began on 1 July 1916.

It started when the vast **Lochnagar mine** (see page 71) – one of 16 such mines laid by the British beneath German lines along the battle front – exploded ten minutes ahead of the 07.30 start. Debris was flung almost a mile into the air, as graphically recorded by Royal Flying Corps pilot Cecil Lewis in his book *Sagittarius Rising*: 'The whole earth heaved and flared, a tremendous and magnificent column rose up into the sky.'

Moments after the explosion of these large mines, the British and French forces emerged from their trenches under cover of artillery fire. Despite inflicting considerable damage on some German strongpoints, progress proved elusive. By the end of the first day, 58,000 casualties were recorded, of whom 19,000 died. These casualties were the largest ever loss sustained by the British Army in a single day.

Spasmodic fighting continued until, with battlefields churned into a muddy morass, the respective armies settled into their winter quarters. After 4½ months, the British had advanced 12km. Of the three million soldiers from all sides recorded as having been sent to the Somme Front Line during this period, some 1.2 million were wounded, killed or went missing in action. To put this into perspective, at the time of writing, 444 British soldiers have been killed since 2001 in the Afghan War.

The Somme Offensive remains one of the most widely remembered battles of World War I, in part because, unlike the essentially Franco-German Battle of Verdun, it involved over 20 nationalities fighting or working on behalf of Great Britain, France and Germany. These included, Russian, Belgian, Chinese and Egyptian forces, individual Americans and, in 1918, American forces, as well as contingents from Montenegro, Romania, Switzerland, Sweden and Spanish Catalonia.

WHAT TO SEE AND DO

Notre-Dame d'Amiens (*Pl Notre-Dame 30;* ☏ *03 22 71 60 50; http://cathedrale-amiens.monuments-nationaux.fr/en;* ⊕ *Apr–Sep 08.30–18.15 daily; Oct–Mar 08.30–17.15 daily; adult/child €5.50/4*) This magnificent 13th-century church, the largest Gothic cathedral in France, miraculously escaped destruction during World War I. Pictures of the cathedral, and notably of the touching sculpture of *The Crying Angel,* regularly featured on postcards that soldiers sent home. Six Allied flags are displayed inside the edifice, while commemorative plaques pay tribute to Field Marshal Foch and General Leclerc and to the soldiers who fought in the Somme.

PÉRONNE

Péronne, a historic town on the Somme River with a medieval castle in the centre, was occupied by the Germans for much of World War I. As a result, the town was frequently bombarded. The French civilians here suffered terribly; almost 30% of residents became victims of the war. The Germans eventually left Péronne of their own accord in March 1917, but recaptured it in March 1918 during their Spring Offensive. It was finally liberated by Australian troops on 2 September 1918.

GETTING THERE AND AWAY Coming **by car** from Amiens, follow the E44/A29 east for 32km, then take exit 53 and merge onto A1/E15/E19 north to Péronne (*66km; 50mins*). There is no **train station** in Péronne.

Notre-Dame d'Amiens (CP/ST)

Chapelle de Souvenir, Rancourt (AD/ST)

WHAT TO SEE AND DO
Museum of the Great War (Historial de la Grande Guerre) (*Château de Péronne;* 03 22 83 14 18; *www. historial.org;* Apr–Sep 09.30–18.00 *daily;* Oct–Mar 09.30– 17.00 *Mon–Tue &* Thu–Sun; *adult/child (6–18)/over 60s €7.50/4/€6.20, €20 family ticket (2 adults & 2 children); suitable for those with physical, mental or hearing disabilities; W/A)* Péronne's Historial de la Grande Guerre is one of the most important museums dedicated to World War I in France. It occupies the remnants of the town's medieval castle, which have been greatly added to by the contemporary exhibition spaces created by architect Edouard Henri Ciriani.

The coverage of the Great War is in good part thematic, and the emphasis is put on the individuals involved in the terrible campaigns. The objects on display are in themselves often telling: for example, a German shovel laid alongside a French one, or a British private's trench clubs, testifying to the brutality of hand-to-hand fighting. Shared grief and competing memories emerge in many depictions, such as bronze carvings, statues and lithographs. The museum holds remarkable war etchings by German artist Otto Dix. Temporary exhibitions are regularly held here, and look out for special displays during the World War I centenary commemorations. The centre also offers group tours of the battlefields and has a **research centre** for those tracing relatives. Contact Caroline Fontaine (03 22 83 54 13; c.fontaine@historial.org).

AROUND PÉRONNE

RANCOURT
The Chapel of Remembrance (*Route National 2;* 09.00–18.00 *daily; free entry*)
This substantial chapel, the one significant monument commemorating the French Army's participation in the Battle of the Somme, was built to remember the French soldiers who died in a violent communications-busting offensive around Rancourt, from September to November 1916. The impetus for the chapel's construction came from Marie Mathilde du Bos, née Johnston, originally from New Orleans. She was the mother of Jean du Bos, one of the fallen. Much of the funding for the building was raised by public subscription in the USA. The largest French cemetery in the Somme spreads out around the chapel. There is a large German cemetery nearby, plus a small British one.

LONGUEVAL
South African National Memorial (*Lies off the D929 towards Calais and Lille, on edge of Delville Wood*) Rows of oak trees grown from South African acorns lead to an arch recalling a terrible week in July 1916 when the 1st South African Brigade spent five nights and six days fighting the enemy in Delville Wood. Of the original 121 officers and 3,032 South African soldiers that fought here, only 142 emerged unscathed.

National Museum and Visitor Centre (*Route de Ginchy 5;* 03 22 85 02 17; *www. delvillewood.com;* Apr–mid-Oct 10.00–17.30 *Tue–Sun;* Feb–Mar & mid-Oct–Nov 10.00–16.00 *Tue–Sun*) Set behind the national memorial, the National Museum, built to reflect South African architectural styles and opened in 1986, recalls in some detail the role played by South African soldiers in World War I. Across the road from the

South African Memorial and Museum stands the large Delville Wood Cemetery, created after the war and mainly containing the graves of unidentified soldiers who died from July to September 1916.

New Zealand Memorial and Caterpillar Valley Cemetery *(New Zealand Memorial just north of Longueval village, along a little road off D197; Caterpillar Valley Cemetery not in Caterpillar Valley, but on south side of D20 between Longueval & Contalmaison; both ⊕ daily)* The Memorial obelisk pays homage to the New Zealand Division's role in the Somme Offensive from 15 September 1916, while the large Caterpillar Valley Cemetery also commemorates Kiwi soldiers who went missing through the Battle of the Somme. The names of 1,205 New Zealand and Maori soldiers with no known grave are engraved on a wall here.

ALBERT

Located on a major route through northern France, the town of Albert has been repeatedly destroyed down the centuries. In World War I it long lay close to the Front and the Germans bombarded it heavily throughout 1915. A German shell badly damaged the dome of the town's great 19th-century basilica, causing the gilded statue of the Virgin on the top to lean precariously, a position in which she was famously left for the rest of the war. The ruined town had to be wholly reconstructed after the conflict; the basilica was rebuilt in its original style.

GETTING THERE AND AWAY Coming **by car** from Amiens, follow the D929 east direct to Albert *(30km; 35mins)*. From Amiens or Arras, **trains** take approximately 20 minutes.

WHAT TO SEE AND DO
The Somme 1916 Museum (Musée Somme 1916) *(Underground, reached from beside the Basilica Notre-Dame de Brebières, Rue Anicet Godin;* ✆ *03 22 75 16 17; www.musee-somme-1916.eu;* ⊕ *daily 1 Feb–30 Mar & 1 Oct–30 Nov 09.00–12.00 & 14.00–18.00, 1 Apr–30 Sep 09.00–18.00, 1–20 Dec 09.00–12.00 & 14.00–17.00;* €6/4

> **TOURIST INFORMATION**
>
> **Albert Tourist Office** 9 Rue Léon Gambetta; ✆ 03 22 75 16 42; http://somme-poppy-albert.jimdo.com; ⊕ Apr–Sep 09.00–12.30 & 13.30–18.30 Mon–Fri, 09.00–12.00 & 14.00–18.30 Sat, 10.00–12.30 Sun; Oct–Mar 09.00–12.30 & 13.30–17.00 Mon–Fri, 09.00–12.00 & 14.00–17.00 Sat, closed Sun

Exhibits at The Somme 1916 Museum (PC/ST)

adult/child, under 6s free) Granted, dioramas and reconstructed scenes cannot recapture the squalor of the war – the mud, the cold and the lice, fleas and rats – but the 250m-long, 10m-deep tunnel at this museum does a pretty good job.

AROUND ALBERT

THIEPVAL Thiepval's role in the Battle of the Somme was a strategic one, with the Germans building a major line of defence around the village. Captured by British troops on 27 September 1916, retaken by the Germans in March 1918, it was finally recaptured by the British in August the same year.

Ulster Tower (DG)

Thiepval Memorial and Visitor Centre (*Rue de l'Ancre;* ☏ *03 22 74 60 47; www.historial.org; memorial:* ⊕ *always; visitor centre:* ⊕ *Nov–Feb 10.00–17.00 daily; Mar–Oct 10.00–18.00 daily; free entry*) The largest British war memorial in the world, the massive Thiepval Memorial to the Missing reaches 45m in height. Designed by Sir Edwin Lutyens and built between 1929 and 1932, it caused controversy when it was constructed because of the cost. Most movingly, its many towering sides are covered with the names of over 72,000 British and South African soldiers with no known graves – the so-called 'Missing of the Somme' – who died in battles between July 1915 and March 1918. However, 90% of those recalled died between July and November 1916. Annual commemorative ceremonies are held here on 1 July and 11 November.

Located a few hundred metres from the memorial, the contemporary visitor centre explains how and why the vast edifice was erected at Thiepval, including via three short films, as well as giving an overview of World War I. Computer databases are available to those researching individual soldiers who died in the war or for those wishing to locate a cemetery or memorial.

Ulster Tower (Tour d'Ulster) and Visitor Centre (*Route de Saint-Pierre-Divion;* ☏ *03 22 74 87 14; www.irishsoldier.org;* ⊕ *May–Sep 10.00–18.00 Tue–Sun; Mar–Apr & Oct–Nov 10.00–17.00 Tue–Sun, closed Dec–Feb*) A replica of Helen's Tower from the Clandeboye Estate in County Down, Ireland, the Ulster Tower marks the spot from where troops of the 36th Ulster Division advanced on a German strongpoint on the initial 1 July 1916 Somme Offensive. They suffered over 5,000 casualties, with approximately one man in four killed, injured, missing or taken prisoner. Nine Victoria Crosses were awarded. The small museum beside the tower gives some further information on the fighting in these parts and has some rare personal items on display.

BEAUMONT-HAMEL This village north of Thiepval, set above the Ancre Valley, had been heavily fortified by the Germans prior to the start of the Somme Offensive.

Newfoundland Memorial and Beaumont-Hamel Visitor Centre (*On route D73 approximately 1.5km southeast of Auchonvillers*) Beaumont-Hamel lay on the northern end of the section of the Front that was chosen for the Somme Offensive, which began on 1 July 1916 (see box, page 66). A massive mine planted by British engineers went off nearby at 07.20 that morning, ten minutes before the assault, rather than two minutes before, like the other mines laid along the line. This early warning, along with the Germans' high position, allowed them to mow down the soldiers of the Newfoundland Regiment as they emerged from their trenches close by. After 30 minutes, only 110 out of 780 men remained unharmed in one of the most devastating actions on the first day of the Battle of the Somme.

After the war, the Dominion of Newfoundland bought the land where the regiment had been stationed and preserved it. Visitors can therefore walk through one of the clearest extant network of trenches. Various memorials not just to the Newfoundland Regiment stand scattered about the park, but none is more striking than the bronze statue of a caribou, the Newfoundland Division's emblem, standing atop a mound looking out towards the German lines. At the base, three bronze plaques commemorate 820 men from the regiment, the Newfoundland Royal Naval Reserves and the Mercantile Marine who died in World War I and whose bodies have never been found.

The **visitor centre** (✆ *03 22 76 70 86; www.veterans.gc.ca;* ⊕ *10.00–17.00 Mon, 09.00–17.00 Tue–Sun; free entry*) traces the history of the Newfoundland Regiment and some of its characters, alongside displays of memorabilia and video snippets.

POZIÈRES As the Somme Offensive evolved through July 1916, Australian troops were heavily involved in the task of securing Pozières, its high, well-defended ridge which was a key obstacle to capturing the vital Thiepval Ridge. In the fierce fighting that month, the three Australian divisions involved lost over a third of their men.

Pozières War Memorials (*along the D929 Albert-Bapaume road*) There are two important Australian memorials at Pozières: one to the 2nd Division at the highest point on Pozieres Ridge, where a windmill once stood, and one to the 1st Division at Gibraltar. On the opposite side of the busy road, the **Tank Corps Memorial** recalls the first-ever use of a tank in battle, at Flers-Courcelette, on 15 September 1916. As to the separate, impressively colonnaded **Pozières Memorial**, it lists the names of 14,692 British and South African soldiers with no known graves who died in the Second Battle of the Somme between 21 March and 8 August 1918. Every two years, Digger Cote 160, an association of local people from Pozières (*www. digger–pozieres.org*), stages war performances in the village.

OVILLERS-LA-BOISELLE
Lochnagar Crater (*www.lochnagarcrater.org*) Caused by British mines set off at the very outset of the Somme Offensive, Lochnagar Crater is on a staggering scale, being 91m wide and 21m deep, making it one of the largest war-time craters ever created. It is looked after by a passionate British man, Richard Dunning, who bought the site in 1978 and allows visitors to see it for free, although he is grateful for donations. A duckboard trail allows you to walk around the rim. Every July, a

Newfoundland Memorial Beaumont Hamel (AB/ST)

Aerial photo of Lochnager Crater (PC/ST)

memorial service is held by The Friends of Lochnagar, chaired by Richard Dunning.

MAMETZ Although the village of Mametz was captured by the British 7th Division on 1 July 1916, further progress was blocked by heavy German resistance in Mametz Wood, which was taken on the 12 July after heavy losses by the 38th Welsh Division.

The Welsh Dragon Memorial of the 38th Division (*from Mametz village, take road towards Contalmaison & follow signs in Welsh to the memorial; www.tourisme-paysducoquelicot.com; free entry*) Inaugurated on 11 July 1987, the monument to the 38th Welsh Division is the Red Dragon of Wales, it wings held aloft and it claws clutching pieces of barbed wire.

LA NEUVILLE-LÈS-BRAY
Little Train of the Upper Somme (*Hameau de Froissy, 80340 La Neuville-lès-Bray;* 03 22 83 11 89; www.appeva.org; ⊕ *May, Jun & Sep 14.00, 15.15 & 16.30; Jul–Aug 14.30 & 16.00 Tue–Sat, 14.00, 15.00, 16.00 & 17.00 Sun; adult/child (5–12)/under 5s €9.80/6.80/free*) Railway buffs enjoy this narrow-gauge line built in 1916 for the Battle of the Somme and used to supply the trenches with weapons. On part of the 30-minute, 14km journey between Froissy and Dompiere, you follow the Somme River itself.

The railway's **museum** at Froissy (⊕ *May, Jun & Sep 13.30–18.00 Sun; Jul–Aug 14.00–17.45 Tue–Sat, 13.30–18.30 Sun*) displays many locomotives and wagons, including French, German and American ones, mostly from the 1910s and the 1920s.

LE HAMEL ON HORSEBACK

Explore Le Hamel and the Australian battlefields by horse and carriage on 1½-hour **tours** (03 22 96 03 16; penseedelehamel.blog4ever.com; €20pp).

LE HAMEL
Australian Memorial (*Chemin de Sailly Laurette, east out of Le Hamel village centre*) This memorial marks the successful battle on 4 July 1918, when General Sir John Monash, one of the most creative and forward-thinking generals in World War I, led his Australian and American troops into a clash that lasted only 93 minutes. Take a look at the German trench as well as the 20 information panels around the site.

VILLERS–BRETONNEUX It was here that Aussie soldiers stopped the German push in April 1918, preventing Amiens from being captured.

Welsh Dragon Memorial (AD/ST)

PERSISTENCE PAYS OFF IN SEARCH FOR UNCLE

Private Alec Reader (DG)

Doug Goodman describes how he traced the spot where his uncle died on the Somme.

The faded photographs of a soldier in uniform, found among old 1920 holiday snaps, had little significance as a child. I only remember being told it was my uncle ' lost in France in the war'. But it was to become very significant indeed.

In the early hours of Friday 15 September 1916, at a spot known as High Wood near the French town of Albert, a whistle gave the signal for infantrymen of the 47th Division to go over the top as Allied forces attempted to capture German trenches along a section of countryside on the Somme.

For Private Alec Reader, the battle was to be the culmination of 13 months' training as a rifleman and bomb-thrower. It was also to be his last chance for action: he was being allowed to leave the army because on the day of his enlistment he was only 17 – four months under age.

The Times talked of the attack as a 'great day for the cause of civilisation' and the *Telegraph* listed several thousand killed and injured. Alec was one of them. His mother received a letter saying his body had been found at the edge of the wood and properly buried.

For years she tried to find out where, but in 1923 the Imperial War Graves Commission told her that although the area had been searched and the remains of soldiers buried, isolated graves had been reverently re-buried in cemeteries and the last resting place of Private Reader remained unidentified.

In 1928 the Reader family visited the Menin Gate memorial at Ypres, seeking Alec's name in stone, but found nothing. A further visit in 1938 to Belgium revealed no trace, and the life and death of Private Reader, No 3623 of the 15th Battalion Prince of Wales' Own Civil Service Rifles, became history.

And that might have remained the case had not his 77 letters home come into the possession of Roger Goodman, his nephew, in 1983. His citations and medals were found, press cuttings and official correspondence assembled, photographs acquired and family memories jogged. Military records were examined and visits to the Imperial War Museum and the Musée de la Guerre in Paris provided valuable information. Old books on the battles and modern then-and-now publications were obtained and battlefield maps and diaries held at the Public Records Office were scrutinised, until eventually the missing details fell into place.

And so it was, on a sunny May morning Roger and I, his younger brother, found our uncle's name, among 73,000 others without a known grave, in the commemorative book and carved in stone on the Thiepval Memorial, less than two miles from the spot where he fell.

There, on the edge of High Wood where the last cavalry charge and the first tank attack took place and where more than 8,000 soldiers died, a monument to the men of the 47th London Division had been erected – and we remembered one of them fondly as we stood in the corner of that little French wood.

Australian National Memorial (*beside D23 road c2km north of Villers-Bretonneux towards Corbie; www.tourisme-corbie-bocage-3-vallees.com; free entry*) Designed by famous architect Sir Edwin Lutyens – who also designed the Thiepval Memorial (see page 70) – and inaugurated by King George VI in July 1938, this memorial marks the 10,982 names of missing Australian soldiers from World War I. The burial places of some of these men have since been identified and research continues to this day; six of them were among the discovery of 250 burials which culminated in the new Pheasant Wood Cemetery at Fromelles (see page 46). An ANZAC-Day Dawn Service is held annually on 25 April (*www.anzac-france.com*).

Franco–Australian Museum (Musée Franco–Australien) (*9 Rue Victoria;* \ *03 22 96 80 79; www.museeaustralien.com;* ⊕ *Nov–Feb 09.30–16.30 Mon–Sat; Mar–Oct 09.30–17.30 Mon–Sat; adults/children & students €5/€3*) Created by the Franco–Australian Association in 1975, this museum is located on the first floor of the town's Victoria School, rebuilt in the 1920s using donations from school children in Victoria, Australia. The collection covers the role of Australia in World War I, plus the flora and fauna of Oz.

DOULLENS

HALL OF THE SOLE COMMAND (*1st Flr of Hôtel de Ville, 2 Ave du Maréchal Foch;* \ *03 22 32 54 52; www.doullens-tourisme.com;* ⊕ *08.00–12.00 & 14.00–18.00 Mon–Fri, 10.00–12.00 Sat; free entry*) It was here on 26 March 1918 that, at the behest of General Haig (see box, page 63), the French and British governments appointed General Foch to take over as Commander in Chief of military strategy. On 8 August he launched his final counteroffensive, which led to the Armistice being signed on 11 November 1918.

CANTIGNY

AMERICAN MEMORIAL (*In centre of the village*) This memorial marks the thousand-plus casualties of the 1st American Division and 28th American Infantry Regiment at the Battle of Cantigny between 28 and 31 May 1918. This was the first major American offensive of the war and not only did it contain the German's Spring Offensive, it also raised Allied morale and showed the competence of the US soldiers, which was further displayed by the American Army and Marine Corps in subsequent campaigns during 1918.

10

Aisne

Overshadowed by the slaughter at the Battle of the Somme (see box, page 66), in fact, Aisne, the Picardy département (or county) east of the Somme, also suffered terrible destruction through World War I, when its wooded landscapes became a permanent battleground. Most atrocious was the protracted conflict between German and French forces for control of the Chemin des Dames Ridge. It was in Aisne that the first trenches were dug in 1914.

LAON

As département or county capital of Aisne, the medieval town of Laon is a good base from which to explore nearby wartime sites. The city remained in German hands throughout the war.

GETTING THERE AND AWAY From Calais **by car**, follow the E15/A26 southeast to Arras, then the E17/A26 continues past Saint-Quentin to Laon (*225km; approx 3hrs*). If travelling from Belgium, follow the E19/A2 west down to Cambrai, then pick up the E17/A26 to Laon (*approx 1hr40mins*). **Trains** depart regularly from Paris Gare du Nord (*1hr30mins*), Reims (*35mins*) and Saint-Quentin (*50mins*).

TOURIST INFORMATION

Laon Tourist Office Hôtel Dieu, Pl du Parvis Gautier de Mortagne, Laon; 03 23 20 28 62; www.laon-tourism.co.uk; 25 Apr–30 Sep 09.30–13.00 & 14.00–18.30 daily, 1 Oct–8 Apr 09.30–12.30 & 14.00–17.30 Mon–Sat, 14.00–17.30 Sun

AROUND LAON
Veslud German Cemetery (*Take the A26/E15 signposted Reims–Paris & continue to Saint-Quentin, then junction13 for N2 & D1044; the cemetery sits beside Veslud Church; www.memorial-chemindesdames.fr*) This communal cemetery contains the graves of 1,704 German soldiers who were buried here after the April 1917 Chemin des Dames Offensive. In 1979, the old wooden crosses were replaced with stone crosses or stelae (inscribed stone slabs).

Saint-Erme Cemetery (*Rue du Monument, Saint-Erme; follow the D1044 south for 11km, then turn left onto the D90 signposted for Saint-Erme. Once there turn left at the T-junction in the direction of Ramecourt & take the second exit marked 'Toutes Directions' & look out for the cemetery sign*) Encircled by a rubble wall, this cemetery is hidden down a 30m pathway off the main road. Look for the Commonwealth War Graves Commission sign at the entrance. An extension of the

AISNE

Cross in Veslud Cemetery (FV/AT)

local communal cemetery, it contains the bodies of 76 Commonwealth soldiers, seven of which remain unidentified. Of these, 36 were moved here from the Ramecourt Communal Cemetery.

Sissonne British Cemetery (*La Garenne des Cheneaux, Sissonne; follow the D1044 for 2.8km, then branch left onto D181 crossing over the E17/ A26 motorway, through Sissonne village; memorial is 1km on right – look for tall white cross*) This small, pretty cemetery was built after the 1918 Armistice to bring together smaller cemeteries created after the bitter fighting at the Chemin des Dames. Today, there are 291 Commonwealth graves here, of which 127 are unidentified. Sissonne was occupied by the Germans throughout the war and next door is a German cemetery which, like the British, is made up of numerous congregated burial sites.

CHEMIN DES DAMES

The Chemin des Dames (*www.chemindesdames.fr; take the N2 & follow the D18 for the main sites*) – now the D18CD road – is a 30km-long route along a narrow and fertile plateau some 50km south of Laon, which rises between the valleys of the Aisne and Ailette rivers. It's here that soldiers of the British Expeditionary Force dug their first trenches on 14 September 1914. For some, it would come to be as relevant to the Great War history as Flanders or the Somme.

Now tranquil, this area is littered with military cemeteries and monuments in honour of the 100,000 soldiers who died fighting over the 100m-high ridge. Famed for its stunning views (you can see Laon cathedral from the top), the Chemin des Dames has seen military action in many periods of history: in 57BC, 100,000 Gauls fought Caesar's legions here; on 7 March 1814, Napoleon fought a battle here; and in September 1914, the Germans – retreating from the fiercely fought Battle of the Marne (see page 86) – used the ridge to create an elaborate system of bunkers and machine-gun nests.

Despite this, and the impregnable nature of the terrain, the French General Robert Nivelle launched the futile Nivelle Offensive in freezing weather on 16 April 1917, in a bid to end the trench warfare. It was originally planned to commit nearly one million men in the battle, including 10,000 Senegalese infantry and 20,000 Russians. It ended in a bloody defeat, with mutinies breaking out in the French Army because of the General's stubborn refusal to call off the offensive. The casualties included 187,000 French and 163,000 Germans wounded, killed or missing. In May General Nivelle was replaced by Marshal Philippe Pétain whose troops captured La Malmaison Fort (see page 79) on the road to Paris on 23 October 1917, leaving the defeated Germans retreating from the plateau to the north of the River Ailette.

WHAT TO SEE AND DO
Dragon's Cavern (Caverne du Dragon) and Chemin des Dames Museum
(*Oulches–La-Vallée-Foulon, off the D18;* \ *03 23 25 14 18; www.caverne-du-dragon. com;* ⊕ *Feb–Apr 10.00–18.00 Tue–Sun; May–Jun & Sep 10.00–18.00 daily, Jul–Aug 10.00–19.00 daily, Oct–Dec 10.00–18.00 Tue–Sun, open public holidays; adult/children (6–18) €6/3, family pass (2 adults & up to 4 children) €15; guided tours last 1hr30mins & depart every 30/40mins in season, tour in English everyday at noon*) In 1914, this site was known as the Ferme de la Creute because it backed onto one of the area's many

TOURIST INFORMATION

The closest tourist offices are located in **Laon** (see page 75) and **Soissons** (see page 80). Information is also available on www.chemindesdames.fr.

old quarries (*creutes*). It was the only position the French would hold on the Chemin des Dames, but on 25 January 1915 it was snatched back by the Germans.

The French were finally able to recapture it on 25 June 1917 using gas, but the following month it was in good part back in German hands, who used it to strengthen their defences. This involved digging new galleries to reach the north of the ridge and installing barracks and a first-aid station with electric lighting.

For several months the opposing forces lived alongside each other in the darkness, spying on each other through a wall built in the galleries. Today, visitors can visit those very same galleries and experience first-hand the (albeit boarded) passageways where, wrote a French soldier, 'one crawls amid unimaginable debris … in a darkness that our lamps could hardly pierce, surrounded by the sickening stench of gas and dead bodies.' There are multimedia tours and a glass-walled reception area with panoramic views over the Aisne Valley. Nearby, a nine-sculpture **memorial** pays homage to Senegalese soldiers who were heavily involved in the fighting.

Monument des Basques, Craonelle (*Chemin des Dames*) Located on a small slip road just off the Chemin des Dames road, this memorial pillar was built in 1928 as a tribute to soldiers of the French 36th Infantry Division who suffered significant losses in the Chemin des Dames fighting in the Plateau de Californie and Craonne area. The architect Mathieu Forest and sculptor Claude Grange were themselves veterans of the war.

Craonne (*From Laon, follow the D1044 south for 18km, then at Corbeny turn right onto D18CD*) The historic village of Craonne was completely obliterated by artillery fire during World War I. Interestingly, the 'Song of Craonne' – written by an anonymous French soldier in 1917 – is still one of pacifism's great hymns. A wooded area marks the start of a 20-minute walk which takes you past the Tree of Peace site, erected by a local school, and offers views over the Plateau de Californie. Pick up a map from the tourist office or download a self-guided PDF map of the Vieux Craonne walk from www.randonner.fr.

Plateau de Californie This 2.5km walk along the Chemin des Dames Ridge is lined with Great War information panels and offers terrific views of the Aisne Valley. Once the site of a farm – dubbed La Californie after its owner left for America to sell champagne – the plateau was the scene of fierce fighting when the Germans launched a surprise attack on British units on 27 May 1918. After the war, not a single tree was left standing. A 25m-high observatory allows you to contemplate the battlefield and see all the way to Reims. You can download a self-guided PDF map of the Belvédère du Plateau de Californie walk from www.randonner.fr.

View of the Chemin des Dames (FXD/AT)

Dragon's Cavern (JD-BAD/AT)

Cerny-en–Laonnois Memorial (*Grande Rue, just off the Chemin des Dames in the village of Cerny-en-Laonnois*) This Classical-style column was built in 1913 in honour of the 1st Battalion of the Loyal North Lancashire Regiment, or 'Old Contemptibles', who on 14 September 1914 captured and held for a brief few hours the heavily defended German stronghold at Cerny Sugar Mill before being forced to retreat.

Vendresse-Beaulne British Cemetery (*Follow the D967 16km south of Laon, the cemetery is 800m north of the village on the west side of the road going towards Laon;* ⊕ *daily; free entry; not W/A*) Located on the ridge flank, this cemetery contains 700 British graves of which only 327 are identified; some simply bear the words 'buried near this spot.' The neighbourhood of Vendresse-et-Troyon saw severe fighting in which British troops took part.

La Malmaison Fort (*Route départementale 18, Chavignon, follow the D18CD;* ⊕ *by guided tour only on the 4th Sunday of each month at 10.30 & 14.30; tickets can be bought from the Dragon's Cavern (see page 77); adult/under 6s €4/free*) Ironically, the fort – one of a string of frontier fortifications built after France's 1870 defeat in the Franco-Prussian war – had been decommissioned in 1912. It was as central to the fighting as Fort de Condé (see page 80).

Driving and Walking Excursions The tourist office has self-guided PDF maps for a 25-minute circular drive taking in the main sights and 12km walks for walkers and mountain bikers, as well as a shorter 20-minute walk.

SOISSONS

Built beside the Aisne River, Soissons is one of the most ancient towns in northern France. It was here, in August 1914, that the British Expeditionary Force crossed the Aisne, and for the next 3½ years, French forces held this part of the Front until it was lost to the Germans in spring 1918. It was recaptured following The Battle of Soissons,18–22 July 1918, involving French and British Divisions and the 1st and 2nd Infantry Divisions (United States), which were under French command.

ANTI-WAR SONG BANNED UNTIL 1974

The *Chanson de Craonne* was an anti-war song that was banned from being sung until as late as 1974. Originally called the *Chanson de Lorette*, it was published under this name in 1919 by journalist Paul Vaillant-Couturier in his book *La Guerre des soldats*. You can see why it didn't go down well: the first verse reads:

Goodbye life, goodbye love
Goodbye to all women,
It's over now, It's over forever
Since this loathsome war.

We have to leave our skins,
On the Craonne ridge,
'Cause we are all doomed to die,
We're the sacrificial victims.

GETTING THERE AND AWAY From Laon **by car**, follow the N2/D23 southwest for 29km then turn right onto N31 to Soissons centre (*approx 35mins*). There are **trains** from Paris Gare du Nord (*1hr15mins*) and direct trains from Laon (*26min*).

WHAT TO SEE AND DO

Monument des Anglais (*Crossroads of Rue Charpentier & Rue du Pot d'Étan; Soissons town centre*) Built in massive white Portland stone and featuring three stout soldiers, this memorial commemorates the 4,000 British officers and men who died in the Battles of the Aisne and Marne in 1918 but who have no known grave. You can see it from outside the low wrought-iron gates, but to gain full access you need to get a digital security code obtainable from the Commonwealth War Graves France Area Office (☏ *03 21 21 77 00;* ⏱ *08.30–16.30 Mon–Thu, 08.30–16.00 Fri*).

Around Soissons

Fort de Condé (*Chivres-Val;* ☏ *03 23 54 40 00; http://english.fort-de-conde.fr;* ⏱ *Apr–May & Sep–Nov 09.30–12.00 & 13.30–17.30 daily, guided tours 14.00 & 16.00; Jun–Aug 09.30–12.00 & 13.30–18.30 daily, guided tours at 14.00, 15.30 & 17.00; adult/10–18/under10s €5/3/free*) Held by the Germans from September 1914 to April 1917, it was here that the French eventually welcomed General Pershing's US troops in their push on La Malmaison Fort. Condé was reoccupied by the Germans at the end of May 1918. They broke through Allied positions in just a few hours, dislodging the French and British soldiers in a deluge of fire. It was to be Germany's last major victory of World War I. By 8 August, the fort was reclaimed by the French 54th Infantry Regiment.

Vailly-sur-Aisne British Cemetery (*13km east of Soissons; the cemetery is on the left side shortly after entering Vailly-sur-Aisne town*) Lying on the north ba nk of the Aisne River, this cemetery contains the graves of 675 British soldiers, as well as bodies from other cemeteries. Of these, 370 graves are unidentified, with 40 headstones showing that the bodies were never found. Though most died fighting along the Chemin des Dames in September 1914, it is also the final resting place for over 60 Commonwealth soldiers who perished in summer 1918.

Carrières de Confrécourt (*Soissonnais 14–18, Farm Confrécourt, Nouvron-Vingré;* ☏ *03 23 55 17 18, or reserve through the tourist office (see above);* ⏱ *Mar–Sep 1st Sun of the month starting at 15.00 in front of the monument of the Broken Cross located on D138 at the village exit towards Saint-Christophe-à-Berry; admission €2*)

La Malmaison Fort (FXD/AT)

Fort de Condé (SL/AT)

These quarries, situated 10km from Soissons, are preserved by the World War I Association Soissonnais. They provided shelter for French soldiers from September 1914 onwards. The quarry walls are engraved with an assortment of graffiti and numerous personal belongings have been found here too. While ploughing his fields, local farmer Jean-Luc Pamart uncovered the bodies of numerous French soldiers who disappeared while defending the line on the banks of the Aisne, and the discovery was part of a BBC documentary. 'The soldiers would be down here for three days at a time,' Jean-Luc told the programme makers. 'So close to the misery and desolation of the battlefields above, and yet they sculpted such magnificent things – and with such limited resources. They were not grandiose works of art,' he added, 'but of the heart, of pure emotion, produced in the most tragic circumstances. Some of them were drawn in pencil but were never finished.' A chapel sits on site too.

Musée Franco-Américain du Château de Blérancourt (*Pl du Général Leclerc;* 03 23 39 60 16; *www.museefrancoamericain.fr;* ⏱ *museum: 14.00–18.00 Mon & Wed–Sun, admission €2.50; gardens: 08.00–19:00 daily, free entry*) Located inside a 17th-century castle, this museum documents the pioneering work of American philanthropist Anne Morgan, who arrived in Blérancourt in 1917 with American women volunteers to carry out relief work for civilians and to rebuild Picardy. The castle was one of five centres she established and her work is remembered via a series of photographs and films kept at the museum.

The museum is also dedicated more generally to the Franco–American relationship in place since the 16th century. It is partially closed for renovation and due to reopen in 2015; check the website before travelling. In addition, you can visit two pavilions: the Anne Morgan Pavilion and the Franco-American Library, the latter open to readers upon written request. Nearby are the contemporary New World Gardens, which are well worth exploring.

Château de Coucy (*Rue du Château, Coucy-le-Château-Auffrique;* 03 23 52 71 28; *http://coucy.monuments-nationaux.fr;* ⏱ *2 May–4 Sep 10.00–13.00 & 14.00–18.30 daily; 5 Sep–30 Apr 10.00–13.00 & 14.00–17.30; admission €5.50, guided tours with reservations*) Various German dignitaries, possibly even the Kaiser himself, were said to have frequented this vast medieval stronghold that was renovated in the 19th century and became a German military outpost on 1 September 1914. In March 1917, the keep and four towers were destroyed, whether for military purposes or merely as an act of vandalism is not known. However, it caused such a public uproar that a month later the ruins were declared 'a memorial to barbarity'. War reparations were used to clear the towers and to consolidate the wall. From the top of the castle you can see for 40km in every direction. Visitors can take a guided tour of the little town of Coucy-le-Château and learn about its occupation during World War I; ask at the tourist office (see opposite page). To get there from Laon, follow the D5 west for 20km (*approx 45mins*).

SAINT-QUENTIN

From 28 October 1914 to 1 October 1918, Saint-Quentin was a logistical hub for the German Army – even the street names were 'Germanised'. During occupation,

Le Pavillion Anne Morgan, Château de Blérancourt (LB)

all means of communicating with the rest of the country were prohibited and the townsfolk were forced to provide food for German troops. Food shortages resulted in deficiencies and disease among the French residents and there were fines for those who refused to comply. Some girls were rounded up to work in brothels, while children were forced to work in the fields or factory workshops.

On 1 October 1918, poet-soldier Wilfred Owen complained in his writings that Saint-Quentin was virtually inaccessible behind its rows of barbed wire – just before the city fell into the hands of French and British troops. They were astounded by what they saw, with 80% of the town destroyed, and only 253 people remaining.

TOURIST INFORMATION

Saint-Quentin Tourist Office Rue Victor Basch 27, Saint-Quentin; 03 23 67 05 00; 1 Apr–30 Sep 08.00–12.00 & 13.30–18.00 Mon–Fri, 10.00–12.30 & 14.00–18.00 Sat, 14.30–17.00 Sun; 1 Oct–31 Mar 08.00–12.00 & 13.30–18.00 Mon–Fri, 10.00–12.00 & 14.00–17.00 Sat, closed Sun

GETTING THERE AND AWAY Saint-Quentin stands alongside the E17/A26 between Arras and Laon. It is also connected directly to Amiens via the E44/A29 motorway. Two fast **trains** depart from Laon each day with a change at Tergnier (*50mins*).

GUIDED TOURS
Paths of History 03 23 67 77 64/06 31 31 85 02; contact@cheminsdhistoire.com. Tailor-made tours based on the life of a soldier, unit, nationality or a specific site, led by World War I expert Olivier Dirson.

WHAT TO SEE AND DO
Monument Pont de Riqueval (*9.5km north of Saint-Quentin off the D1044*) On 29 September 1918, Captain Charlton of the British 1/6th North Staffordshire Regiment and soldiers in the Royal Engineers blocked this bridge, foiling German attempts to blow it up, granting the Allies control over the canal area around the village of Bellenglise. A photo taken of the fighting by an official British war photographer, David McLellan, can be seen at London's Imperial War Museum.

Around Saint-Quentin
Somme American Cemetery and Memorial (*Quennemont; 1.5km southwest of Bony;* 09.00–17.00 daily; free entry) This cemetery pays tribute to the vital role Americans played in Aisne. Stark white crosses mark the graves of 1,884 US servicemen who were killed while serving in units attached to the British Army. The outer walls of the chapel, whose large bronze doors sport an America eagle, feature sculptured pieces of military equipment.

TOURIST INFORMATION

Château-Therry Tourist Office Rue Vallée 9; 03 23 83 51 14; www.chateau-thierry-tourisme.com; 10.00–12.30 & 13.30–17.00 Mon–Wed & Fri–Sat, 11.00–12.30 & 13.30–17.00 Thu, 13.30–17.00 Sun & public holidays

CHÂTEAU-THIERRY

Château-Thierry stands at a strategic point on the Aisne River between Paris and Reims. It experienced heavy fighting in 1918, particularly between American and German troops.

GETTING THERE AND AWAY If coming **by car,** Château-Thierry lies off the E50/A4 motorway linking Paris and Reims (*1hr 10mins*). Direct **trains** from Paris Gare de L'est take 50 minutes; trains from Reims take about one hour.

WHAT TO SEE AND DO
American Monument, Hill 204 (*Rue de la Côte 204;* ⊕ *09.00–17.00 daily; free entry*) This imposing granite monument overlooks the Marne River valley and is a mark of American–French friendship. The Hill 204 monument commemorates the US soldiers who died in the Aisne–Marne Salient in 1918. Visitors can learn about the battles from the orientation map on the monument.

Aisne–Marne American Cemetery (*At the entrance of Belleau, see below;* ✎ *03 23 70 70 90;* ⊕ *09.00–17.00 daily; free entry*) Sits at the foot of the famous Belleau Wood battlefield. The cemetery contains the graves of 2,289 US soldiers, most of whom fought in the vicinity during the summer of 1918.

Musée de la Mémoire de Belleau 1914–1918 (*Pl du Général Pershing, Belleau;* ✎ *03 23 82 03 63; www.musee-memoire-souvenir-belleau.com;* ⊕ *May–Nov 14.00– 17.30 Mon, 10.30–12.30 & 14.00–17.30 Fri–Sat, 14.00–18.00 Sun; free entry*) This intriguing museum of memorabilia has a special significance for the US Marine Corps who fought in the Battle of Belleau Wood and suffered heavy losses.

OISE

Oise is the third département to make up the Picardy region. In summer 1914, German troops flooded through here to try and take Paris, although they would crucially be pushed back during the First Battle of the Marne (see page 85).

The name of one of Oise's main historic southern cities, Compiègne, would go on to become doubly famous for its links to the history of both World Wars. On 11 November 1918, French, British and German commanders met in a part of the forest east of town that could be reached by rail; they gathered in this secretive spot to sign the Armistice ending the Great War. The Clairière de l'Armistice, or Clairière de Rethondes, therefore became one of the most hallowed of places to the people of France and many others. After a stint in Paris, the railway carriage in which the meeting occurred was moved back to Compiègne Forest in 1920. A memorial museum opened there so visitors could see the carriage and learn about the armistice.

However, at the beginning of World War II, following the lightning German occupation of France in 1940, Hitler rushed to the exact same spot in the Forest of Compiègne to humiliate the French with the signing of a new Armistice heralding Germany's crushing domination of the country. The memorial museum was erased and the Führer had the historic railway carriage taken to Berlin, where it would be destroyed on Hitler's orders in 1945. However, a similar wagon, which was rebuilt after World War II, now stands within the old-fashioned but absorbing Musée de l'Armistice.

Marne, Champagne and Verdun

Along with Flanders and Picardy, an arc of land stretching east from Paris via Reims to Verdun became another of the most terrible theatres of conflict throughout World War I. This arc notably included sections of the Marne and Meuse valleys.

The name of the Marne is indelibly associated with the heroic defence of Paris from invasion in September 1914, and the saving of France from very swift capitulation to Germany. As to Verdun on the Meuse, it has the same resonance for the French as the name of the Somme for Britain and the Commonwealth, witnessing as it did another of the most destructive battles in the history of humanity.

Visiting these parts in the context of World War I, the pleasures of bubbly Champagne seem far removed, yet some uplifting war tales stand out, such as the celebrated story of Paris taxi drivers ferrying soldiers to the First Battle of the Marne, a small but psychologically important part of the war effort. Soldiers of many different nationalities, including British, Commonwealth and American troops, fought in battles from the Marne to the Meuse, and of course the losses for the Germans would be immense.

MEAUX

Museum of the Great War (Musée de la Grande Guerre) (*Rue Lazare Ponticelli, Meaux;* \ *01 60 32 14 18; www.museedelagrandeguerre.eu;* ⊕ *May–Sep 09.30–18.30 Mon & Wed–Sun; Oct–Apr 10.00–17.30 Mon & Wed–Sun; admission €10/7/5/free adult/over 65s & war veterans/child (under 26)/under 8s)* Located above the town of Meaux northeast of Paris and close to some of the main locations of fighting in the early stages of the First Battle of the Marne, this museum is a rich curtain-raiser to exploring the wide-ranging social upheavals brought about by the war to end all wars. Inaugurated appropriately at 11.00 on 11 November 2011, it focuses on the personal lives of those who took part, as well as the military or political issues. At its heart is a collection of 50,000 objects collected over a period of 40 years by photographer Jean-Pierre Verney and bought by the regional councils, who also agreed to provide a massive high-tech museum to house the collection. These items include uniforms, prosthetic limbs, barbed wire, gas masks and a host of other wartime paraphernalia. One gallery shows objects carved and shaped in the trenches, from erotic reliefs cut into the brass casings of shells to bullets turned into salt shakers. One section focuses in

Village de Fleury near Verdun Memorial (VT)

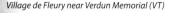

detail on the different stages of the First Battle of the Marne. There are two routes through the museum: the first takes 90 minutes, the other either a half or full day.

REIMS

The major historic city of Reims, on the Vesle River north of the Marne Valley, contains one of the most important medieval cathedrals in France, while celebrated Champagne vineyards lie close by. However, at the start of World War I, the town found itself on the route of German forces sweeping down from Belgium and the Ardennes towards Paris, 129km (80 miles) away. Germans occupied the city from 4–13 September 1914. Thanks to the counteroffensive of the First Battle of the Marne, the French Army quickly retook Reims, but German troops then stationed themselves in forts surrounding the town. As a result, the city suffered devastating bombardments for 3½ years. The cathedral alone was hit by almost 300 shells. Reims lay 60% in ruins by the conflict's end, and 740 civilians had lost their lives.

TOURIST INFORMATION

Reims Tourist Office 2 Rue Guillaume de Machault; ☏ 0821 61 01 60 (€0.11/min); www.reims-tourisme.com
Regional Tourist Information www.champagne-ardenne-tourism.co.uk

GETTING THERE AND AWAY From Calais **by car**, follow the E15/A25 south to Arras and then pick up the E17/A26 to Reims (*272km; approx 2hrs30mins*). By **train**, take the TGV, which departs regularly from Paris Gare de L'Est (*45mins*).

WHAT TO SEE AND DO
La Main de Massiges Trenches (*South of Reims; signposted from village of Massiges;* ⊕ *daily; free entry*) This mind-boggling network of trenches and fortifications is being restored to its original condition on a hilltop near the village of Massiges. From September 1915 to September 1918, fierce trench warfare took place here (during the two battles of Champagne), with trenches changing hands between enemies several times. Seven bodies – six French soldiers and one German – were discovered in 2012 and 2013. They have since been buried in local military cemeteries.

Vallée Moreau German Rest Camp (*Route 63, between Vienne-le-Château & Binarville;* ☏ *03 26 60 49 40;* ⊕ *Jan–May & Oct–Dec 09.00–noon Sat; Jul–Sep 09.00–noon Sat & 14.00–17.00 Sun; adult/under 12s €5/free*) This fascinating collection of trenches, tunnels and buildings has been slowly restored by the Franco–German Committee since 1966. The rest camp was designed to hold several hundred 'off-duty' soldiers, and visitors can experience the daily life of the troops. Interestingly, when construction started in 1915 it was supervised by a young junior officer called Rommel – the future World War II Field Marshal.

Marne 14–18 Interpretation Centre (*4 Ruelle Bayard, Suippes;* ☏ *03 26 68 24 09; www.marne14-18.fr;* ⊕ *Feb–Jun & Sep–Nov 13.00–18.00 Tue–Sun; Jul–Aug 10.00–19.00 Tue–Sun, closed Dec & Jan; adult/6–18/under 6s €6.50/3/free*) Located on the former Front, this museum contains masses of original photos and first-hand accounts from soldiers and civilians.

The pivotal **First Battle of the Marne** was fought between 5 and 9 September 1914. The Germans were nearing the outskirts of Paris in their bid to occupy France, but six French armies and one British regiment engaged them in battle along a wide section of the River Marne and beyond and won. The Germans were forced to retreat to the northeast and abandon their push on Paris – the delay lost them their swift victory over France and set the stage for four years of trench warfare.

The **Second Battle of the Marne** took place between 15 July and 5 August 1918 and was the last major German offensive on the Front during World War I. German forces attacked the French around Reims. However, when American troops and a British Corps joined the French, the Germans were overwhelmed. The German defeat marked the start of a relentless Allied advance that culminated in the Armistice being signed about 100 days later.

Navarin War Memorial (*D977, between Souain & Sommepy-Tahure;* ⏱ *03 26 66 82 32;* ☉ *memorial: daily, chapel: Mar–mid Oct 14.00–18.00 Fri) 10.00–12.00 & 14.00–18.00 Sat–Sun & public holidays; free entry*) Located in the heart of the Champagne battlefields and topped by a sculpture depicting three soldiers, this monument commemorates the fighting of October 1914 and September 1915. The surrounding land still bears the scars of heavy conflict.

La Pompelle Fort (*D944, direction Châlons-en-Champagne*) This fort was built in 1880 as one of a ring of defence points around Reims. During four years of heavy shelling in World War I, it was the only citadel around Reims to remain in the hands of the Allied forces (French and Russian troops). A monument that symbolises the city's resistance against the invaders, the fort has been converted into a war museum housing a rich collection of artefacts.

It's currently closed for extensive renovations, but is due to reopen in July 2014 – ask Reims tourist office for updated information.

St-Hilaire-le-Grand Russian Chapel and Cemetery (*D21, L'Espérance;* ☉ *cemetery: daily, chapel: 15 Apr–15 Nov 15.00–17.00 every other Sunday; free*) This Russian chapel is dedicated to the 6,100 Russians who, among the troops sent over by the Tsar, died in France. The adjacent cemetery is the final resting place for around 1,000 Russian soldiers.

Memorial of the Battles of the Marne, Dormans (*Parc du Château, Dormans;* ☉ *1 Apr–11 Nov 14.00–18.00 Mon–Sat, 10.00–12.00 & 14.00–18.00 Sun & public holidays; free entry*) One of France's four French national memorials, it looks out over vineyards and the River Marne, and commemorates the two Battles of the Marne, which occured in 1914 and 1918. The memorial comprises a crypt, chapel and ossuary containing the remains of over 1,000 soldiers of mixed nationalities.

Monument of Mondement (*D45, between Oyes & Broyes; www.mondement1914. asso.fr/english;* ☉ *monument: daily, museum: Jun–Sep 15.00–18.00 Sun*) This monument in the hamlet of Mondement-Montgivroux commemorates the First Battle of the Marne and is located at a strategic point in the conflict. The accompanying Mondement History Museum is housed in the former village school.

Marfaux British Cemetery (*D386, between Dormans & Reims*) This Commonwealth cemetery contains the graves of 1,114 British soldiers and 15 New Zealanders.

VERDUN

The name of Verdun, a significant small city on the Meuse River in the northeastern French region of Lorraine, is inextricably linked with one of the most appalling wars of attrition ever pursued by opposing forces. The Battle of Verdun in 1916 (see box, page 88) became the longest battle of World War I. Over 300,000 French and German soldiers died and over 400,000 were wounded within an area of only 20km². The so-called Red Zone, the area at the heart of the conflict, still bears its terrible scars.

GETTING THERE AND AWAY From Reims **by car**, follow the E17/A4 southeast towards Châlons-en-Champagne, then pick up the E50/A4 near La Veuve (*121km; approx 1hr15mins*).

WHAT TO SEE AND DO

Underground Citadel (Citadelle Souterraine) (*Ave du 5ème RAP;* 03 29 84 84 42; www.citadelle-souterraine-verdun.fr; www.meusetourism.com; ⏲ Feb & Dec 10.00–12.00 & 14.00–17.00 daily; Mar, Oct & Nov 09.30–17.30 daily; Apr–Jun & Sep 09.00–18.00 daily; Jul–Aug 09.00–19.00 daily, closed Jan; adult/child (8–16) €7/3.50, €19 family ticket (2 adults & 2 children)) Dug between 1886 and 1893, these galleries depict the lives of French soldiers who were stationed here. The 45-minute tour concludes with an historical reconstruction of the ceremony honouring the Unknown Soldier (see page 45).

The Verdun Memorial (*1 Ave du Corps Européen, 55100 Fleury-devant-Douaumont;* 03 29 84 35 34; www.memorialdeverdun.fr; ⏲ Jan–Feb & Dec

Exterior of the Underground Citadel (JMP/VV/VT)

Fought over the course of ten months, between 21 February and 18 December 1916, the Battle of Verdun was initiated by the Germans, who wanted to deal the Allies on the Western Front a crushing blow by capturing Meuse Heights and the French-held fortified town of Verdun – a vital gateway town on the way to Paris. It was arguably the most influential battle of the Great War.

On 21 February, the Germans began by bombarding French lines for over 21 hours. Progress was slow, but four days later they captured Douaumont fortress. After some early gains in territory by the Germans, however, fierce retaliations by the French led the battle into a bloody stalemate, and the conflict became a devastating battle of wills – fighting for fighting's sake over an area of just 20km^2 with a few metres being gained and then lost.

Calculations from historical documents suggest that there were over 70,000 casualties for each month of fighting, with approximately 542,000 French and 434,000 German casualties – close to a million casualties in total – making it one of the longest and costliest battles in human history. Historians estimate that 40 million artillery rounds were expended during the battle. The German defeat marked the start of a relentless Allied advance that culminated in the Armistice being signed about 100 days later.

10.00–12.00 & 14.00–17.00 daily; Mar & Nov 09.30–12.00 & 14.00–18.00 daily; Apr–May 09.00–18.00 daily; Jun & Sep 09.00–18.30 daily; Jul–Aug 09.00–19.00 daily; Oct 09.00–12.00 & 14.00–18.00 daily; adult/8–16/under8s €7/3.50/free, €18 family ticket: 2 adults & 2 children) Lying at the heart of the battlefield, some 4km from Verdun, this memorial is one of Europe's principal Great War museums. However, it's closed for major renovation and due to reopen in November 2015 in time for the commemoration of the Battle of Verdun (see box, above).

The memorial also has a **Documentation Centre** (🕐 09.00–12.00 & 14.00–18.00 Mon–Fri), which is open to everyone. They prefer for you to make research appointments two weeks in advance, but call to check if the opening times have been affected during the museum renovation.

Douaumont Ossuary and Necropolis (55100 Douaumont; 📞 03 29 84 54 81; www.verdun-douaumont.com; 🕐 see website for details; admission to ossuary: adult/child 8–16/concessions/military €5/3/3.50/2.50, under 8s free) Officially opened by President Albert Lebrun on 7 August 1932, the Douaumont Ossuary contains the remains of 130,000 unknown French and German soldiers who died at the Battle of Verdun. The 137m-long cloister has tombs in pink granite with bones collected from all 36 areas of the battlefield. With 204 steps, the 46m-high tower contains a war museum in the middle. Unveiled on 29 June, 1929, the necropolis stretches out in front of the ossuary with orderly rows of 15,000 crosses, the largest French necropolis of the Verdun battlefield and an immensely humbling sight.

Appendix 1

FURTHER INFORMATION

BOOKS There are hundreds of history books that cover the four-year war. These are a collection of the most authoritative and/or accessible.

Taylor, AJP *The First World War: An Illustrated History* Penguin Books, 1974. This classic textbook guide to the First World War is concise, but Taylor's style is rather dry in places and his opinions biased and largely out of date now. However, the numerous photos and diagrams still make it a worthwhile read.

Paxman, Jeremy *Great Britain's Great War* Viking, 2013. Brings to life what war was like for everyone, from the politicians and Tommies to wives and nurses.

Strachan, Hew *The First World War*, Free Press, 2006. Academic work by one of the world's leading Great War expert.

Howard, Michael *The First World War: A Very Short Introduction* Oxford University Press, 2007. Ideal, quick read to understand the basics.

Stevenson, David *1914–1918: The History of the First World War* Penguin, 2012. Very thorough coverage written by London School of Economics' International History Professor.

WEBSITES
World War I

www.greatwar.co.uk
www.greatwarcenetenary.be
www.greatwarjourneys.com
www.flandersfields.be
www.flandersfields1418.com
www.rememberancetrails-northernfrance.com

Tourist Information

http://wartimehistory.pas-de-calais.com (Pas-de-Calais)
www.greatwar14-18.co.uk (Aisne)
www.toerisme-ieper.be (Ypres)
www.tourisme-nord.com (Le Nord)
www.somme-battlefields.com (Somme)
www.visitflanders.co.uk (Flanders)

Giving something back

www.nfassociation.org The Not Forgotten Association provides recreation for wounded, injured or sick ex-servicemen and women.
www.cwgc.org Commonwealth War Graves Commission maintain memorials and graveyards across France and Belgium.

Travel

www.accessibleflanders.be Information for disabled travellers
www.delijn.be Public transport network in Flanders
www.belgianrail.be Booking website for all train travel in and around Belgium
http://en.voyages-sncf.com Booking website for all train travel in France

GLOSSARY

ANZAC	Australian and New Zealand Army Corps
British Expeditionary Force	British Army deployed to the Front
W/A	Wheelchair accessible

Index